T0208284

This Journal Belongs To

. . . .

Wife of Law Enforcement Officer

. . . .

Date Journey Began

. . . .

Moments of Truth

An Inspirational Journey for Wives of Law Enforcement Officers

Jessica Kay Mertz

WESTBOW
PRESS®
A DIVISION OF THOMAS NELSON
& ZONDERVAN

This book is a work of non-fiction. Unless otherwise noted, the author and the publisher make no explicit guarantees as to the accuracy of the information contained in this book and in some cases, names of people and places have been altered to protect their privacy.

WestBow Press books may be ordered through booksellers or by contacting:

WestBow Press
A Division of Thomas Nelson & Zondervan
1663 Liberty Drive
Bloomington, IN 47403
www.westbowpress.com
1 (866) 928-1240

Because of the dynamic nature of the Internet, any web addresses or links contained in this book may have changed since publication and may no longer be valid. The views expressed in this work are solely those of the author and do not necessarily reflect the views of the publisher, and the publisher hereby disclaims any responsibility for them.

Any people depicted in stock imagery provided by Getty Images are models, and such images are being used for illustrative purposes only. Certain stock imagery © Getty Images.

Scriptures taken from the Holy Bible, New International Version®, NIV®. Copyright © 1973, 1978, 1984, 2011 by Biblica, Inc.™ Used by permission of Zondervan. All rights reserved worldwide. www.zondervan.com The "NIV" and "New International Version" are trademarks registered in the United States Patent and Trademark Office by Biblica, Inc.™

ISBN: 978-1-9736-6312-6 (sc)
ISBN: 978-1-9736-6314-0 (hc)
ISBN: 978-1-9736-6313-3 (e)

Library of Congress Control Number: 2019907103

Print information available on the last page.

WestBow Press rev. date: 08/27/2019

To the amazing wives of law enforcement officers, bless you.

To the law enforcement officers who serve and protect us, thank you.

To my favorite officer, Dan, I love you.

Contents

Preface
How to Use This Book

● ● ●

There's just something exciting about beginning a journey and embarking on an adventure, whether that's starting a new job, getting married, having kids, moving, or going on a vacation. Whatever journey it is, it helps us grow as a person and it might even help shape us into the individual we were meant to be.

Some journeys we get to plan and we know what we're getting ourselves into. We are able to work out the details perfectly. Others, though, are set before us and we might find ourselves on paths that we didn't expect, with no input from us. These are the journeys that can be incredibly hard at times—but later, we know they were worth it and greatly strengthened us.

That's how this book evolved. The first few years my husband was a police officer (as well as a military police officer), I knew I needed to find a way to encourage myself. I did it through journaling, highlighting verses in my Bible, saving quotes, and jotting down some of our family's stories. I did all these things to keep ME going. I was doing it ALL just to help myself—and then God laid it on my heart to share my journey with YOU, my friend.

When you think about it, anytime you go on a new adventure it's always better, more comforting even, to have a friend with you. I want to applaud you for choosing to join me on this inspirational journey. For that's what this book will be—a time for us friends to dive in, get to know each other, and share our journey as wives of law enforcement officers together.

I strongly believe the topics covered in this book will encourage and aid you to be a better law enforcement officer's wife (which I'll refer to as LEOW going forward). I'm sure you are quite amazing already but I feel we can all improve in order to help our law enforcement officers (which I'll refer to as LEO going forward) in this troubled world, as well as help ourselves with any worry and stress that comes with our husband's duties.

Ladies, I designed this book with YOU in mind. I tried to make it user-friendly and convenient. Over the next month, I encourage you not only to focus on how you can support your husband but also on who *you* are as a LEOW. What do you do well? What areas do you want to grow on this journey?

I'm sure you are a busy woman because most LEOWs are—working, running the household, and possibly raising children. Therefore, I only want it to take ten to fifteen minutes to work through the "Moments of Truth" sections of the book. Look at it as a small investment of your time, one to help you become a more supportive LEOW. My wish is that you will do this for yourself in your important role as a LEOW.

No matter how religious you are or which church denomination you come from (or even if you don't attend church or are on the fence about God), I know this book will guide you through relevant topics to help you, your LEO, and your family. I also felt it would be helpful to provide any Bible verses I reference in the text. I don't know about you, but having to flip back and forth between two books takes too much space and time. I have used the New International Version (NIV) of the Bible for most of the verses but encourage you to also use your own preferred translation so you can read and highlight, if you wish. Or, consider downloading a Bible reading app to go deeper in your faith.

Personally, I like lists, making a plan, and being organized when going through a devotional or journal. This approach helps me in my thought process and hopefully will help you as well. I've organized each day with the following structure:

- **Title** - something catchy to help you remember the topic
- **Verse** - a small portion of Scripture relevant to the day's topic
- **Reading** - a page of stories and thoughts to help guide you
- **Prayer** - a short prayer you can use to connect with God on the day's topic
- **Moments of Truth** - questions and areas of reflection for you to complete
- **Action items** - a place where you can apply the topic that was covered

Finally, before you begin, I want you to know that I did not hold anything back, my friend. Because of this, some readers might feel I'm being a bit crude or brash, but I promised to tell the truth, the whole truth, and nothing but the truth, so help me, God! I promise I will be open and honest with you, and trust me, I will be more *real* with you than I am with some of my own friends and family. In return, I want— no, *I need*—you to be real and honest with yourself and to tell the truth so that you will get the most out of this journey. Don't hold anything back—really dive in!

I encourage you to set aside some time in your day, find a quiet spot, read and focus on the day's topic, and do the activities, all of which will help you in your important role as a LEOW. Best wishes on this journey of working through your own moments of truth. Let's get started!

Introduction

We live in a troubled world. Some of you are already saying, "Amen!" We know firsthand what our officers deal with and that sin is among us and is increasing. We, more than the average citizen, know the negative things that are happening not only in the world and nation but also in our very own communities. This is a hard burden to carry. LEOs deal with murders, domestic violence, substance abuse, rape, child abuse, theft, and even more horrific crimes on a daily basis all while they go about their jobs of protecting and serving. I'm sorry to say this evil is not going away nor is it going to get any easier.

Before writing this book, for about a year, I held a position as the mayor's administrative assistant and I enjoyed the fact that every day was different. While at the office, I answered and screened phone calls. It seemed simple enough, but I could never predict what type of call or caller I would be dealing with. Would they need information about a city department? Was it a media request? Was a citizen checking the status of something happening in the community? Or was it something else?

The one type of call I did not like but often received were from angry people. It was normal for me to hear complaints from unhappy citizens—even though we were in a pleasant city. I became good at empathizing with the caller and showing concern while trying to determine the specific person they needed to talk to, because not everyone needs to speak to the mayor about their issue. The reason many people called the mayor was that they did not know who else they could talk to. They had exhausted all other measures and now felt they needed to take it to someone who was higher up the ladder, so to speak, and who would take action.

Of all the calls I dealt with, the ones I disliked the most were complaints about law enforcement. Callers would sneer, "Police are corrupt!" "I'm being targeted by the cops!" "They have nothing better to do than stalk me!" "They are useless!" I heard all types of negative comments, some of which had more colorful language than I care to share with you, my friend! It was hard to listen to because I usually knew the officer they were referencing, or knew enough about the situation, to know the accusation was false. I can confidently say we have a wonderful police and sheriff department made up of strong leaders and outstanding officers.

I concluded that the real problem is the growing lack of respect for the authority of LEOs in our society. Current events receiving heavy media coverage do not help the situation. I think everyone who reads this would admit that the past few years have been a turbulent time for law enforcement agencies all over the United States. Even peaceful towns such as mine in the Midwest have felt the ripple effect. It's a scary world at times. And it's easy to get overwhelmed with the negativity. That is why God wanted me to share my journey with you. I wrote this book to encourage and to help you, so you, in turn, can encourage and help your LEO. But before we go any further, I want to pray for you and your officer.

My Prayer for Your Officer

Dear God in Heaven,

I pray specifically for the LEO of the loved one who holds this book. Thank You for the position You have put him in and for the specific calling You have placed on his heart. Bless him for serving those who may not appreciate him and protect him from those who may try to cause him harm. Please shield him from all evil, guide him in his actions, and bring him home safely to his wife and family who love him. Amen!

Your Prayer for Your Officer

My Prayer for You

Father in Heaven,

I thank You for the woman about to embark on this journey. I pray that You will give her the time to focus on the topics, readings, and activities. Please help her as she works through her own moments of truth with honesty and sincerity. Lord, please encourage her when she feels discouraged or tearful when troubles come her way. May You guide and help her in this important role, so in turn, she can better support and serve her LEO. Amen!

Your Prayer for Yourself

Day 1

Lord, Help Me! I'm in Love with a LEO!

1

Lord, Help Me! I'm in Love with a LEO!

* * *

*Trust in the Lord with all your heart and lean not on
your own understanding; in all your ways submit to
Him, and He will make your paths straight.*

Proverbs 3:5–6

Lord, help me! I'm in love with a LEO!

Please let me clarify this statement. I am not referring to the astrological sign called Leo, the Lion. (Although I'm told it's hard to love them at times because of their need to be center stage!) I also do not mean that I cannot believe I still love my husband. I do admit we have had our share of challenges over the years and that some days are definitely easier than others. What I do mean, and what surprises me the most, is that I am actually married to someone who is in law enforcement.

I do not know if you have had similar thoughts, but during the past nine years that my husband has been an officer with the Rapid City Police Department, I have found myself thinking, *I can't believe the man I fell in love with and married is a police officer.* On these days, I have to remind myself of the path that got us here. I never planned to be married to someone in this field. We were already married and had children when my husband chose this path in life or, rather, when it chose him.

Some of you knew what you were getting into. You crazy ladies! Maybe when you started dating, you knew what his career was. Maybe your love story was something from a scene in a movie. He pulled you over and you flirted a bit. A week or so later, you ran into each other at the grocery store, started dating, and had the fancy wedding. The rest is history. Others of you married into the law enforcement family because someone introduced you to each other. Maybe your own father or brother was in law enforcement, and you were already part of the "Thin Blue Line" family.

No matter what journey or path got you here, most of you are like me. Your husband felt called to this position, and therefore, you had to wrap your brain around this new life change and adjustment. I had to do this and I'll be honest, it was difficult at times.

I had my doubts and even asked my husband if he was 100% sure this was what he wanted to do. I experienced fear and uncertainty along with a skewed view of what LEOs do. However, I knew that if God wanted my husband to be in this role, He would take care of him as well as my fears and insecurities. I had to trust and not lean on my own understanding, just as the Bible states.

I have since learned that some of the best LEOs have diverse backgrounds. I know some amazing officers who were once missionaries, teachers, professionals, business owners, and soldiers. They bring these life experiences with them and in turn, this makes them better servants of the law.

I know that I am indeed in love with a LEO! You and I love and stand by our men in whatever they do, even if our own minds do not understand the paths they have chosen to take. We can rest assured that God knows our paths and promises to make them straight. Therefore, we will deal with the life God has given us and try to be the best LEOWs we can be. We will love our officers and support them daily, no matter what that looks like.

A Prayer

Lord, help me to trust You with my life and my husband's life. Help our family in this important role You have placed on us. Help me to love my LEO more today than I did yesterday.

Moments of Truth

Was your husband in law enforcement when you first met him? If so, describe how you met.

If you were already married when your husband decided to become a LEO, what were your thoughts?

How have you and your husband changed since you first met and fell in love?

Please write down any additional thoughts or comments.

Today's Action Item

To Do: Surprise my LEO by saying, "I love you" out of the blue and just because.

I can also:

Day 2

Everyone Loves a Man in Uniform, Right?

2

Everyone Loves a Man in Uniform, Right?

* * *

Finally, be strong in the Lord and in His mighty power. Put on the full armor of God, so that you can take your stand against the devil's schemes.

Ephesians 6:10–11

It was a frigid day as I marched in a Veteran's Day parade, proudly holding up my sign with frozen fingers: "I LOVE A MAN IN UNIFORM!" My husband has worn many uniforms during our time together, ranging from those of a security officer, a soldier, and now a police officer. Truth be told, I love him in all of them.

Seriously, who doesn't love a man in a new uniform? They look sharp and leaner; they stand taller; they appear stronger and in a position of authority. I confess that I love a man in uniform! (Insert my squeal of excitement here.)

Sometimes when I see my husband in uniform, especially if it has been a long time since I've seen him in one, he takes my breath away. I feel so proud of all he has accomplished and that he is mine. Sometimes I just want to tear that uniform off him and drag him into the bedroom—he looks that good—but I will save that conversation for another day! On other occasions, I've felt mixed emotions upon seeing my spouse in his uniform. Perhaps it's because it reminds me of the possible danger he could encounter.

I've heard from other wives that they do not like to see their LEOs in uniform at all. It is a turnoff because they look stiff, cold, or even distant. Or maybe when they see them in uniform, they may think of the way sweaty Kevlar smells—yuck. I don't know what it is, but some wives don't like the look one bit.

I cannot imagine having to wear such a uniform. It must be such a burden to wear each day. No wonder my husband asks me to rub his back when he comes home and finally sheds the layers and the stress.

Maybe you often see your LEO in uniform. He may be dressed before he leaves for his shift. Maybe you rarely see your LEO in uniform because he chooses to get dressed at the station or leaves for work while you are away or are still asleep. Even if you don't see your LEO on a daily basis in uniform, I imagine you have proudly displayed pictures of him around your house or have a favorite photo saved on your phone.

Some of us get so used to seeing our husbands in uniform, we forget the effect that uniform has on others and how important it is to our officers' safety. When someone who is in uniform walks into a room, what happens? All attention is immediately on that person. He is in charge; a level of authority is established. LEOs need this in their positions and in the many situations they encounter.

The uniform also protects them and holds their gear. Just as soldiers fit themselves before a battle, our LEOs fit themselves for whatever may occur that day or the battle we hope they will never have to fight. It is strange to think of your husband armored for battle, but that is what he does when he puts on his uniform. Let us not become lackadaisical and forget the point of it all.

I feel it is also important to remember that many other people do not like our LEOs' uniforms. The way they look may cause uneasy feelings or even fear. However, even those who don't like the uniform can't deny that it sets LEOs apart and puts them in a position of authority and control.

I've learned how important the uniform is over the years. At times, I have loved it, and at other times, I have hated it. But however we feel, we cannot deny that it makes a LEO different, sets him apart, and makes him ready to stand against the presence of wickedness in humanity—in whatever form that might come.

I'm just glad my man looks sexy while ready for battle. I might as well enjoy one of the perks, right?

A Prayer

Lord, help me to respect the uniform that my husband wears. Just as he fits himself with his gear, help me to put on my spiritual armor as well.

Moments of Truth

Do you remember the first time you saw your officer in uniform? What were some of your feelings and thoughts?

How often do you see your husband in uniform or in *work* mode? During these times, does he look different to you from when he is at home? If so, how and why?

Why is the uniform important to you and your LEO? How do you show it the respect it deserves?

Please write down any additional thoughts or comments.

Today's Action Item

To Do: Wash and iron my LEO's uniform for him.

I can also:

Day 3

Cookies with the Rookies!

3

Cookies with the Rookies!

●　●　●

*"For I know the plans I have for you," declares
the Lord, "plans to prosper you and not to harm
you, plans to give you a hope and future."*

Jeremiah 29:11

I have a theory. I believe you can tell a lot about a person by the cookie they eat. For example, the person who chooses an oatmeal raisin cookie goes for the healthy choice and plays it safe. An individual who chooses a white chocolate macadamia nut cookie is a unique individual and usually stands out from the crowd. The person who grabs a chocolate chip cookie is an all-American. Lastly, a person who boldly takes a double chocolate chip cookie is someone who lives life to the fullest. Like my theory?

When my husband first started his career as a LEO, his department held a gathering so we could meet the other rookies, their wives, and their families, as well as some of the brass within the police department. At this small celebration and graduation party, they served cookies and we nibbled and visited. It was a great idea!

Before this moment, I didn't truly know what being a police officer entailed. There were no handy manuals or guides such as *Cop Wives 101* or *Cop Wives for Dummies*. I sure wish there would have been! I remember thinking, *Why doesn't someone write a book to help with all the jargon, lingo, call numbers, and codes?* It was a foreign world and new language to me. I needed help to understand everything.

Some of you can barely remember the feelings of being new and lost. Others of you are brand new LEOWs and are reading this in hopes of getting a glimpse of what you can expect. Regardless of the place you are at, it is important that you are an interested wife and ask your husband questions such as, "How was your day?" "What's going on in the big city?" "Anything new at the department?"

You definitely don't want to be a naive LEOW who thinks all her husband does during a shift is write speeding tickets or, on the other extreme, only deal with murders. There are so many various aspects of the job. It is important for you to learn about them so you can be an engaged and interested wife. I would encourage you to look for avenues and opportunities to learn about your husband's role and his department.

The Rapid City Police Department offers a program called Citizen's Police Academy, and I had the privilege to attend it. It taught me the many facets of this profession and was an excellent way for me to get involved. If something like this is available to you, I highly recommend you get your butt there! The investment of your time and energy will definitely be worth it.

However, if something like this is not available in your area, I encourage you to do your own research, go on a ride-along, read books, join other police wives' Facebook pages, look into the resources available to you, and attend department orientations, programs, and other functions it hosts. Do not only rely on cop shows or action movies to get your information. They are not real, nor are they a healthy way to understand what your husband's workday is like. It is exciting to learn something new. Look at it as if you are also a rookie and do your own private investigation.

Above all, instead of worrying about what the future might be for us and our LEOs, we should remember that God is in control. We can do our part by learning more and being involved. I once heard that knowledge can replace fear, and I have found this to be true. Once I understood more about what my LEO did on a daily basis, and how well-trained he was, I became less fearful. I took the attitude that, "God's got this, so I am not going to worry." Instead, I'm going to eat a cookie . . . or two!

A Prayer

Thank you, Lord, for having the best plans for us. Help me to be supportive of my husband's position and to be well educated about what he does. Please provide opportunities for me to learn more about his role.

Moments of Truth

How much do you know about your husband's agency, department, and position?

What can you do to learn more?

In what ways does today's verse about trusting God's plan apply to you and your family?

. . . .

. . . .

. . . .

. . . .

. . . .

. . . .

. . . .

. . . .

. . . .

. . . .

Please write down any additional thoughts or comments.

. . . .

. . . .

. . . .

. . . .

. . . .

. . . .

. . . .

. . . .

. . . .

. . . .

Today's Action Item

To Do: Ask my husband to tell me about one unique part of his job.

I can also:

Day 4

What's a Few More Brothers?

4

What's a Few More Brothers?

• • •

*A person standing alone can be attacked and defeated, but
two can stand back-to-back and conquer. Three are even
better, for a triple-braided cord is not easily broken.*

Ecclesiastes 4:12

Here's a little bit of info about me: I was raised by a single mother and had only one sister, so the male world was completely foreign. It was a much different world for sure! Now, it is strange to live in a guy's house with guy's stuff and listen to guy's talk. Ladies, I'm sure you agree—our LEO's gear is everywhere!

When my husband became a LEO, our family grew with the addition of a few extra brothers. No one prepared me for these extra "relatives" and all the pizza, beer, and guns that would come with them. They call it a brotherhood, but I refer to it as a gang! I have learned that no matter what happens, they need to connect because they cover for each other.

I love today's verse and the visual it gives. I can imagine two officers standing back-to-back and ready to fight. Then a third officer steps in to make them even more unstoppable. Frodo said in the *Lord of the Rings*, "Frodo wouldn't have gone far without Sam." He wouldn't have gone far without the Fellowship, either. I think this is true for many of our LEOs as well. They would not get far physically, emotionally, or even spiritually without the help, support, and heckling of their brothers in blue.

The majority of LEOs do not have work partners with them on a daily basis, so they need as much support and assistance as possible from one another when serious situations arise. They have to be ready to step in, at a moment's notice, for their brothers, and in return, they rely on their brothers when needed. They know that if they need each other, they will be there. They will be ready to stand back-to-back and, if necessary, to fight.

I realize I cannot be everything to my LEO. He needs time with the guys. As his wife, it is important that I ensure he has guy time and that I don't become jealous of it. He needs time to connect with his co-workers, chat about things only they can relate to, go to a movie, have a drink, watch a game, play some ball, or take a hunting trip. Whatever they do, this time is important and vital for them if they are to build relationships and trust. It also gives them a place to let off some steam.

For a while, my husband and a few LEOs would meet monthly at a bar and grill for a "Bible study" late at night. I was reluctant and even a bit snippy about it until I realized that it *was* a Bible study even if they had beers and ate wings while they chatted. My husband told me they were opening up and talking about what was on their minds. I then realized the importance of this time and knew it was important for my husband to bond with his brothers. So I put on my big girl panties and did not get upset when I had to share him one night out of the month.

You can foster positive LEO family time by hosting opportunities for the guys to hang out. Chances are, they will bring their wives, girlfriends, and families along so you can connect with them as well. When my husband was fairly new, these barbecues and pizza nights got us through some uncertain times. When our officers were tired and stressed, we survived and grew because we had had these moments together.

Now, on the flip side, if your LEO spends every spare moment with his buddies, there might be a problem. However, if it's normal guy time, let him have it. He needs it, and you need it too, unless you want to eat wings, drink beers at midnight, and talk about gory incidents. I would prefer to save myself from the heartburn and let him go hang out with his posse.

A Prayer

Lord, thank You for the extra brothers You've placed in my husband's life. Help them to be there for each other and to build each other up. Help me to be their sister in Christ and to be understanding of their guy time.

Moments of Truth

What does brotherhood mean? What does it look like?

Who are your husband's co-workers? Do you know them and their families? Are they good influences?

What can you do to foster a healthy relationship with your husband and his brothers?

Please write down any additional thoughts or comments.

Today's Action Item

To Do: Invite a LEO family over for dinner.

I can also:

Day 5

Get Some More Sisters!

5

Get Some More Sisters!

* * *

*Finally, brothers and sisters, whatever is true, whatever
is noble, whatever is right, whatever is pure, whatever
is lovely, whatever is admirable—if anything is excellent
or praiseworthy—think about such things.*

Philippians 4:8

Previously we talked about how our LEOs need brother time. Well, ladies, today we are going to cover our need for quality sister time.

I am blessed to have a biological sister whom I love and is truly a friend as well. Even though we live miles apart, we talk every few days. I am thankful that her guidance and humorous wit are just a phone call away.

I have also been blessed with a spiritual sister who has been there for me through everything since first grade and is practically family. She has seen me at my worst and best times and has loved me the same through them all. Without her, I do not know if my relationship with Christ would be as strong as it is.

We all have close relationships, whether they are with relatives or friends. I feel it is also important that we have strong friendships with other LEO wives, since they can relate to our specific struggles and understand our challenges. I love having close friends in my life who are in a similar place and really get me.

At times, I thought it would be beneficial to have a sister wife to share life with! The idea fascinated me. Who hasn't watched the show and imagined what life would be like with a sister wife? I could cook and work while she cleaned and raised the babies. While sharing the family responsibilities and having a sister all of the time sounds like a good plan, sharing the husband is what gets me. (Insert the sound of tires shrieking here.) I do not think I would be good at that. Nope!

Couldn't do it. I do not foresee a sister wife in my future. (Plus, it is illegal!)

However, the idea of going through life with someone and having a sister you can vent to and be there for would be ideal. For that reason, I strongly believe in establishing a sisterhood—a strong support group among LEOWs. It is not only important but necessary. If there already is a group associated with your husband's department or agency, I strongly encourage you to get involved or to attend a meeting. However, if no group has been established, I challenge you to step up and start one, or at least get a few of you together.

This might be hard for some of you. You might be an introvert or live in a community where there are not many LEOWs with whom you could connect. I encourage you to pray that a sister will come into your life, and I pray that you can take the first step by asking someone to meet for coffee or lunch. I don't even drink coffee but love it when someone asks me to join them. I do not need the caffeine to give me a boost because the friendship and the fellowship are enough.

Here are a few things I have done with other LEOWs that drew us closer: attended a book club or Bible study, cleaned up graffiti, cooked for the homeless mission, served the elderly, had a game night, met for a movie, and took a painting class. Once you get together and do a few things, your relationships will grow naturally. I have also found that the less-structured events usually become the best times to truly connect.

Lastly, today's verse is a great reminder to avoid gossip and the negativity that can be found in many women's circles. Let your sister time be positive and uplifting! I promise life will be better if you have a couple of sisters to go through this journey with. I'm so thankful for all of my RCPD sisters. We've shared laughter, tears, and many vent sessions over the years.

A Prayer

Thank you, Lord, for the other LEOWs who have become my sisters. Help us to connect so we can be there for each other. Help me to be a positive light in our group as we support our husbands. Please give us opportunities to serve You.

Moments of Truth

Who are the LEOWs you can count on like a sister and who counts on you?

....

....

....

....

....

....

....

....

....

....

How can you foster growth and relationships among fellow wives?

....

....

....

....

....

....

....

....

....

List some ideas that you and other LEOWs could do together in your community:

Please write down any additional thoughts or comments.

Today's Action Item

To Do: Ask a LEOW to meet for coffee.

I can also:

Day 6

So ... What Does Your Husband Do?

6

So . . . What Does Your Husband Do?

● ● ●

The one who has knowledge uses words with restraint,
and whoever has understanding is even-tempered.

Proverbs 17:27

"**S**o . . . what does your husband do?" Ah, it's the question to end all questions. It's the *big* one that comes up in conversations, especially when I meet someone new. I've got the question, "What do *you* do?" covered. However, when that person asks about my husband, it gets a bit trickier. I always have to weigh how much I should tell the person who is asking. It seems as if it should be an easy enough question to answer, but at times it can be very difficult depending on the occasion. There have been a few situations when I did not want to disclose that he was a city cop. At other times, I could not disclose it for some reason or felt it was not necessary for those around me to know what he did. In those instances, I would give a quick answer, "He works for the city." And, hey, it's not a lie!

Sometimes keeping quiet is the best thing to do. At other times, the person could even be testing you. Some people already know what my husband does because they have dealt with him or recognize him or our last name. In my experience, these are the more difficult situations to maneuver through. Another challenge we have encountered is my husband not being treated with respect due to some prior situation.

I am thankful that the general public usually supports officers, but that is not always the case everywhere we go. There are establishments we no longer frequent because they have had prior run-ins with the law, my husband knows they employ criminals, or they have been the scene of a crime he had to attend to. Unfortunately, you and your LEO will go through some of these awkward situations. I can think of a couple that are worth sharing.

One happened at a get-together with friends at a restaurant. My husband ordered a drink, and when it arrived, his—and only his—was horrible. Everyone else's drink was fine and came just as they had ordered it, but his was *bad*! It turns out the bartender had recognized him from a prior arrest. We joked that the drink had something extra special in it, and my husband didn't touch it again.

Another time, we were celebrating our anniversary out to dinner. We were at a nearby town, but the waitress had fought with my husband during an earlier situation a few weeks before. Talk about awkward! We didn't know if she recognized him but made sure our conversation was generic when she came to our table and checked on us. We again tried to look at the situation with humor and said that if she had recognized him, the steak was probably extra good since she had probably spit on it.

It can be a struggle to keep quiet, especially when others disrespect or mistreat the man you love. However, remember that silence is sometimes necessary. The Bible tells us there is a time to keep silent and a time to speak up. I would encourage you to be careful with what you say and to also have an answer ready for the question, "So . . . what does your husband do?" in case a sticky situation should arise. I also encourage you to establish a code word or safe plan in case your husband is ever approached by a criminal who knows who he is and puts both of you in an unsafe place.

A Prayer

Lord, help me to hold my tongue and to use discernment in situations where others want me to reveal what my husband does. Also, let me know when I'm being tested.

Moments of Truth

What is your response when someone asks what your husband does and you don't feel comfortable telling that person the truth?

Write about a time when you felt uncomfortable revealing your husband was a LEO, or when someone (such as a criminal) recognized him as an officer.

How did it make you feel and why?

Please write down any additional thoughts or comments.

Today's Action Item

To Do: Talk to my LEO about a "safe" word in case a situation would arise.

I can also:

Day 7

Want to Go on a Date?

7

Want to Go on a Date?

* * *

*Make my joy complete by being like-minded, having
the same love, being one in spirit and of one mind.*

Philippians 2:2

We love Italian food and have it at least once a week. Lasagna, spaghetti, spaghetti pie, cavatina, chicken Alfredo, carbonara… am I making you hungry? One evening, I made a special dinner (the works) complete with a new pasta dish, garlic bread, steamed green beans, and a salad. I thought my husband would be happy to have this kind of meal for dinner. However, that was not the case. We sat down to enjoy the feast, and he said, "Would you mind if I had a bowl of cereal instead?" You see, he had only been awake a short time because he was currently working the night shift. The kids and I had already had a full day and were ready for our big Italian dinner.

It was difficult for us to be "like-minded" and "one in spirit" when we did not see each other that often because we were going in different directions, following different schedules, and eating at different times. "Be flexible," quickly became our new family motto. We found that we had to actually schedule times to connect with each other. We had dates while the kids were at church on Wednesday evenings and met often for breakfast. Ladies, together with your LEO, determine what time works best for you. Even then, a last-minute call can derail your plans. Again, you must be flexible. Thanksgiving may no longer be on Thursday. Birthdays are sometimes celebrated on a different day.

I was warned that shift work was hard to plan around. Once I experienced it firsthand, I learned that it was not only hard but sometimes impossible to plan anything. Over the years, we have learned to be more spontaneous. When time allows, we go for ice cream, meet for coffee, or snag a quick snuggle. I cannot be frustrated with my husband when he misses things. Instead, I need to readjust my plans and—you guessed it—be flexible.

Becoming a better planner has helped me in this area as well. I have developed a system that seems to work and keeps us all sane and on the same page. We have a family calendar on our fridge. This simple system tells everyone what nights are free, who works when, who has activities, and so on. I would encourage you to find a system everyone in your household can follow. Maybe you will have to synchronize your phone calendars or have a weekly family planning meeting. Do whatever is necessary to get on the same page, be of the same mind, and find time for each other in your hectic lives.

Unfortunately, no matter what you do or how hard you try, this may be difficult to accomplish. You will get frustrated, especially when your LEO is new to his department, has a special assignment, or his shift changes. However, I promise if you remain flexible, keep your lines of communication open, and find time for little moments together, you will get through it. I believe this is the secret to our successful relationship. Since we don't spend much time together, we don't get sick of each other's company. We treasure these moments, even if they are at random times.

So instead of serving so many Italian dinners, we adjusted to having "brinner" (breakfast for dinner) on the menu more often. This seemed like a good compromise to us. Many might find it weird, but it is common for my LEO to have a beer with us while we eat breakfast since he just got home and off his shift. We just go with it. I know you can too. Don't get mad at him if plans change last minute or you're stood up on dates, but breathe, be forgiving, and, you guessed it . . . be flexible!

A Prayer

I need time with my LEO, Lord, and he needs time with me. Please help us to be like-minded. When schedules become difficult, help us to appreciate the simple moments we have together and to be more flexible.

Moments of Truth

In what ways can you make the time you have with your husband more meaningful?

. . . .

. . . .

. . . .

. . . .

. . . .

. . . .

. . . .

. . . .

. . . .

. . . .

When is the best time for both of you to connect with each other?

. . . .

. . . .

. . . .

. . . .

. . . .

. . . .

. . . .

. . . .

. . . .

What family systems do you have in place to help you be of one mind?

Please write down any additional thoughts or comments.

Today's Action Item

To Do: Try a new recipe for dinner.

I can also:

Day 8

Boys and Their Toys

8

Boys and Their Toys

• • •

For where your treasure is, there your heart will be also.
Matthew 6:19

Normally, I don't host product parties. I know so many people who are consultants of various products, I could host a party every week if I wanted to. I made a rule early on to support other people's home parties by buying only a couple of items from each one and not to host a party myself.

However, I broke my rule. I met someone who sold a new line of jewelry that I *had* to have. I was interested in half of the items in the catalog, so the consultant convinced me to host a party. It was a fun night of desserts, wine, and tons of jewelry. It was a success because of the rewards I earned. In addition, I bought tons of stuff to get me to the next reward level. I know you understand what I'm talking about. I blew my monthly budget on bangles. Seriously, girls, it was BAD!

My husband gave me a lot of grief about this event. He joked for weeks that he was going to host a guns and ammo party for the guys and blow part of the month's budget on accessories for his guns.

I don't know about you, but I can sure spend money. I can also do a great job of sticking to our budget when I need to. But somehow, I can always find a few extra dollars in the budget for a pair of cute shoes. My problem is that I buy a lot of cheap items. Twenty dollars here and there can add up and play havoc on a budget.

My husband, on the other hand, is not a shopper. We joke that he makes the money and I spend it. However, when he wants to buy something, it *has* to be the newest, best, top-of-the-line item. I specifically remember one time when he said he was going to buy new tennis shoes after work. I understood that. A person who is a runner needs new shoes more often. But when I saw the amount he spent for them, I nearly fell out of my chair as I balanced our account. I could have bought five pairs of shoes for the amount he spent on one pair that would soon become stinky sneakers.

Honest and open conversations about spending money and having a budget are necessary in a marriage. Once you establish a set amount, you will not have to feel guilty about spending money because you will have a guideline and avoid disagreements. Arguing about finances is one of the top problems couples face. Why add any more stress to our marriages?!

I've seen issues arise when LEOs feel entitled to buy big and fancy toys. LEOs drive fast, new cars at work, so they want a nice vehicle at home. They use the newest and highest quality guns and equipment at work, so they want the newest models for personal use. When they have time off, they want all of the tools they feel they need to fix house projects. When they have free time for their hobbies, they want the best gadgets and gizmos. This can be a *big* issue for everyone but especially for LEOs.

I am not a financial planner but can honestly tell you this: fighting with your spouse about finances will never go well and fighting with a LEO makes it even worse. Can I get an "Amen!"? For the peace and financial security of your family, you need to work together when it comes to your budget. Many helpful resources and tools are available. I highly recommend that together you take a class, go through a workbook, or meet with a financial planner to get on the same page.

A turning point early on in our marriage was when my husband and I attended a Dave Ramsey Financial Peace class offered by our church. Dinner was potluck style and childcare was provided. It was so convenient we couldn't pass it up. During this class, we made a conscious team effort to get out of debt and to start a financial plan. We have had setbacks and have failed at times, but all in all, we are moving forward financially. In turn, we can give back to God and bless others. It is a good place to be. And meeting financial goals is so much better than bickering over purchases.

A Prayer

Lord, thank You for the resources You have given us and for providing for our needs. Help us to control our wants and give us a grateful spirit.

Moments of Truth

In your relationship, who is the spender and who is the saver?

Do you and your husband have a financial plan and budget that you have both agreed on?

What are some ways that you give back to God?

Please write down any additional thoughts or comments.

Today's Action Item

To Do: Review and update the budget with my husband.

I can also:

Day 9

Keeping the Dinner Conversation PG

9

Keeping the Dinner Conversation PG

• • •

Do not let any unwholesome talk come out of your mouths,
but only what is helpful for building others up according
to their needs, that it may benefit those who listen.

Ephesians 4:29

One summer evening, we hosted a barbecue for some of our police family. The weather was perfect. The food that everyone brought was delicious. Almost everyone invited could make it, and the kids were able to run outside and enjoy the beautiful evening. Little did I know, our perfect atmosphere was about to be derailed. The previous night, there had been a serious and, to the LEOs, exciting situation involving a few of the officers who were present. Everyone was eager to tell their side of the story and to hear what went down.

It's common for our family dinner conversations to include the story or call of the day. I hear parts of the story in the news or on social media and usually want to know the rest. But on this particular night, we did not need to hear the unpleasant details. The conversation quickly turned south, and by south, I mean negative and in the gutter. Soon I heard shouting and swearing. Another wife said, "Little ears!" to remind the guys of the kids who were nearby and probably listening.

Our kids, though, are a bit older and are used to it. They know that their daddy and his buddies' stories sometimes might include foul language or graphic scenes. Our kids are so used to it they can find these stories more entertaining than they should and might want to share them with their friends.

Once, our daughter missed school when we went on vacation, so her teacher gave her a journal to write in as an assignment. When she was ready to turn it in, I looked it over. I was embarrassed by one of her answers "What was your favorite memory from vacation?" She wrote, "My daddy telling us funny stories about drunked people!" Thankfully, her teacher knew her daddy was a LEO! Clearly, that wasn't something most first graders would write after a fun-filled family vacation to Disneyland.

Since our LEOs deal with many negative situations and interesting individuals, it is only natural that they want to share and talk about their day with you and their friends. I suggest you come up with key phrases for when the conversation moves from PG to PG-13 and maybe even to R. I might say something like, "Do we have to talk about this now?" or "How about you guys finish that conversation outside on the patio?" Using key phrases to change the conversation will definitely help keep things on a more positive, uplifting note.

I have also learned that, at times, my LEO will want to tell me about some call he went on or something he dealt with that I might not want to know more about. I think it is okay to tell our LEOs that we would prefer not to know all of the gory information. Encourage them to talk to their co-workers or other men in their lives instead.

Another wife shared this story with me. Right before they got ready for bed, her husband shared a lot of details about a case. She was a bit shaken but listened and was supportive. Later, she got moisturizer in her eye, and her LEO thought she was crying. After that, he was always more careful of what he told her, especially before bed. Even though she was tough enough to handle it, it reminded this LEO that his wife was a bit more sensitive than him. He realized that he should leave out some of the details or call another officer.

Maybe you like all the details, or maybe you don't. Either way, just communicate with your LEO so he knows he can share with you at the level you feel comfortable with.

A Prayer

God, please help us in our conversations, especially during family time, so they may be wholesome and pleasing to You.

Moments of Truth

What favorite on-the-job stories does your LEO like to tell?

When is it appropriate for your husband to share his shoptalk and when is it not appropriate?

How do you graciously communicate with your husband that the topic or conversation is not appropriate or wanted at the moment?

Please write down any additional thoughts or comments.

Today's Action Item

To Do: Ask my husband to tell me a funny story from his shift.

I can also:

Day 10

Handcuff Me!

10

Handcuff Me!

● ● ●

I belong to my beloved, and his desire is for me.
Song of Solomon 7:10

I could not believe that we didn't have a key! Normally, they were lying around in various places. I had looked everywhere my husband usually stashed them. I even had friends help me look. We needed to find one quick. My daughter was starting to sense our urgency, and I did not want her to panic. Reluctantly, I realized I had to call for help. She had decided to try on her dad's handcuffs—when he was out of town (of course!). She had put them around her feet, and they were tight.

I first tried calling a few officer friends. No luck! They were either busy, not answering their phones, or out of town as well. She was crying now. I humbly dialed the department's non-emergency line (there was *no* way I was calling 911), and they sent an officer working on our side of town to our house. He arrived in a matter of minutes and saved the day.

This incident was a good reminder to talk to the children again about not messing with their dad's work things. Later on, we were able to laugh about the situation. What we laughed most about was that before help arrived, I had received a funny text from another LEO: "Please tell me they aren't the fuzzy pink kind of handcuffs." Now, that would have been even more embarrassing!

I cannot confirm or deny that I own a pair of those or that we haven't misused my husband's handcuffs before. One time I took boudoir pictures for my husband while he was deployed. It is amazing what hair extensions, fake eyelashes, and a push-up bra can do. I know my husband enjoyed his unexpected gift, especially since it was unlike anything I had ever done for him before. Later he told me that he hadn't even noticed I was holding his Glock and handcuffs until he examined the picture a bit closer another time. His attention had been elsewhere.

Ladies, I warned you that I was going to be open and honest, and what better subject to prove that than the topic of sex? A healthy sexual relationship is important. You and your LEO need to find time for intimacy. We have already established that they look hot in their uniforms but barely have time to eat a meal with the family. When and where are you going to fit in a good shag?

In our husbands' line of work, they might see other women naked. My husband has assured me, though, that it's not the ones he would prefer to see. I have seen strange ladies' names and numbers written on my LEO's hand and found notes in his pockets. Again, it is all part of his job. When my husband worked nights, ladies flirted with him. He even got the nickname Officer McDreamy. No one wants to hear that her husband is getting hit on by drunk ladies, but I assure you, we do not need to get jealous. Instead, let us make sure our LEOs are "taken care of" and that our relationships stay connected emotionally and sexually to strengthen and protect our marriages.

We hold a unique place in our husbands' hearts. We are set apart by God. I can honestly speak from my relationship that not every night will be filled with fireworks. Sometimes, exhaustion, busyness, and not being in the mood will put a damper on the evening's plans. Whatever it is, even if it's just something silly like needing to shave your legs, be open and honest with each other about it. There might be times when the sex is not as spicy as usual, but I encourage you to stay connected. Those times will pass, and before you know it, you might be asking him to get his handcuffs . . . so you can use them on him! Just make sure you have a key handy when it's all over!

A Prayer

Help me to be a confident woman with a strong physical connection to my LEO. Guide us in our intimacy. Help us to be one.

Moments of Truth

How would you rate your current sex life?

What can you do to make it better or to spice it up a bit?

How can you become more confident in this area?

Please write down any additional thoughts or comments.

Today's Action Item

To Do: Shave my legs and make a move tonight!

I can also:

Day 11
Everyone's Nightmare

11

Everyone's Nightmare

* * *

Greater love has no one than this:
to lay down one's life for one's friends.

John 15:13

Have you ever had a dream that was so real that when you awoke, you swore it really happened? Or do you have reoccurring dreams that haunt you? A while back, I kept having the same nightmare, and when I woke up, I was shaking and unable to go back to sleep.

At the time, we lived outside of town and our place was difficult to find. I joked that the only people who ever visited were family members, friends who had been there before, or the Schwann's delivery man. Even now, we live in a quiet place with only occasional traffic noises in the distance. This is where my imagination and fears come into play.

I dream my husband is working. I am lying in bed, the kids are fast asleep, and even the dog is snoring. I hear a car pull up, two doors shut, and multiple people come to our front door, which no one uses (everyone uses the side door). Then, I hear a knock at the door, but it strangely does not wake up the kids or the dog. I get out of bed, pull on a robe, and when I get to the door and look out, I can see the police chief and my husband's lieutenant looking very sober. I become stricken with fear and short of breath and run back to my room, hide under the covers, and never answer the door.

I have had this dream dozens of times. Sometimes it isn't the chief of police but a military official. Sometimes it is his captain and the department's chaplain. Sometimes I hide in the pantry. Sometimes I hide behind the couch. Every nightmare is slightly different, but one thing is always the same. I never answer the door. I already know what they are there to tell me—something has happened to my husband.

This reoccurring nightmare reveals my biggest fear and seems to pop up when I am nervous, under stress, or after my husband has been involved in a confrontation. I pray I never have to walk this dream out in real life. I often pray for protection over my husband and his co-workers.

Unfortunately, dozens of loved ones will walk through their worst nightmare as more and more LEOs are killed in the line of duty every year. We hear how officers give themselves in the line of duty as the ultimate act of service, but deep down, we pray that it is not our LEO, our friends, or our department or agency.

I vividly remember the first funeral we attended for a fallen brother. As his call numbers were announced one last time, you could have heard a pin drop as everyone held their breath. It was the longest moment of silence I had ever experienced. It was a brother's end of watch. It was hard to witness the attending officers in their uniforms, trying to be strong while their hearts were breaking. It really did feel like a nightmare. I know some of you understand this feeling. Your LEO family has felt a great loss and we hold you in our prayers. For those of you who do not know this feeling firsthand, I hope and pray you never have to.

The Bible repetitively tells us, "Do not fear." I have been told this phrase is mentioned 365 times—one for each day of the year. We cannot live in constant fear that something might happen to our LEOs. To be honest, something could happen to any of us at any time. None of us are guaranteed tomorrow. Instead, we must be prepared for the worst and always have hope. That is why I feel it is important to hug and kiss your LEO before he leaves for his shift. Do not see him off in the middle of an argument. Find a way to lay it aside. In case something should happen while he is working, we do not want to have any regrets. Instead, let us go about our lives confidently trusting that God's special hand of protection is on His servant and remember that God says, "Blessed are the peacekeepers."

A Prayer

God, I pray a shield of safety over my husband and all those in the thin blue line family. Help me not to fear but to have confidence in Your protection.

Moments of Truth

Do you and your spouse have an up-to-date will?

Do you know your husband's wishes should anything happen to him? Does he know your wishes or are they written down?

Are you prepared for the worst but always have confidence that God will protect your LEO?

Please write down any additional thoughts or comments.

Today's Action Item

To Do: Squeeze my LEO extra tight before his shift.

I can also:

Day 12

When I Grow Up, I Want to Be Like Daddy!

12

When I Grow Up, I Want to Be Like Daddy!

* * *

Start children off on the way they should go, and even when they are old they will not turn from it.

Proverbs 22:6

Kids are so cute. I love their enthusiasm for life. I especially like how little boys want to be the "man" when they grow up. Whether it is X-Men, Spider-Man, Batman, Iron Man, or Superman, they want to change the world. Then their desire moves to firemen or policemen when they understand that superheroes do not exist—or do they?

I remember my son's excitement when my husband first became a police officer. Every night, he said in his sweet little voice, "Catch me a bad guy tonight!" It was the cutest request, and he made it very clear to everyone that he wanted to be just like his daddy when he grew up.

Even if you do not have children, I am sure you have witnessed kids' reactions to your LEO. They find him, his gear, and his vehicle quite exciting—like something right out of a movie. This excitement is good for several reasons. First, it provides opportunities for our LEOs' gentler spirits to surface, which naturally happens around kids. Secondly, it is important that kids see officers as their friends and people they can talk to and trust. An officer once told me that a parent said to his kid in his presence, "Be good, or he'll take you away." The officer made it very clear that he did not take away kids but only adults who were bad. He wanted the child to know that officers were people kids could trust.

A while back, a little girl asked my husband if he ever arrested kids. Sensing her uneasiness, he grinned and said, "No, we love kids and like to give them hugs." She was happy and hugged him. I love hearing how LEOs positively impact kids: an officer buying an underprivileged kid a bike, an officer giving his packed lunch to a scared kid whose parent had just committed a crime, or an officer taking a troubled teen out for ice cream and a chat. Positive stories like these occur every day. Unfortunately, they are not the stories that hit the news.

I don't know how your LEO interacts with kids. Maybe he is a natural because he has kids of his own or enjoys time with other kids in his life. Or, maybe kids are not his expertise. Whatever the case, kids are the future, and it is important that they have a positive view of law enforcement. You can help support and encourage your LEO in this area because you know best how he reacts to children.

It is odd how time changes things. My son still likes to watch Batman movies but no longer wants to be a superhero or an officer when he grows up. His attitude has shifted a bit. He does not ask his dad to catch a bad guy anymore either. Maybe the excitement has worn off. Maybe he has seen the downside of the job, or maybe he feels resentment that the job sometimes takes priority over his position as a son. Whatever the case, we still encourage him to be supportive and understanding of his father's role, even if this is not what he wants to become in the future.

Maybe you are now dealing with kids who do not want to have anything to do with your husband in his position as a LEO. Maybe they are having problems with individuals who are in authority. They may even be rebelling and testing boundaries. We can still teach our kids to respect authority and those in a position of service. This will make them better citizens in the future. Someday, I'm confident they will look back and appreciate all your LEO has done for them and others.

A Prayer

I pray specifically for our officers when dealing with children. I also pray for my LEO and the kids he will come in contact with. May he be a good role model to them and show them Your love through his words and actions.

Moments of Truth

Who are the kids in your LEO's life and how do they view him?

What is one of your LEO's strengths when he deals with children? What is something you can help him work on?

If you have kids, are they in the stage where they want to be just like their daddy or have they moved to the other end of the spectrum? Why?

Please write down any additional thoughts or comments.

Today's Action Item

To Do: Say positive things about my LEO's work when I am around kids.

I can also:

Day 13

Anyone Up for Donuts?

13

Anyone Up for Donuts?

* * *

I can do all things in Him who strengthens me.
Philippians 4:13

It was too early for my husband to wake me up. I am *not* a morning person. If you wake me before the sun comes up, you better have a really good reason—like going to an amazing garage sale or heading out on a road trip. My husband was shaking me gently. The house was quiet, and the kids were still asleep. My first thought was, *What do you want?* My second thought was, *Not now!*

Finally, I was awake enough to talk and crawled out from under the covers. Like a little kid, he asked, "Do you wanna go get donuts?" I laughed at him, but donuts, especially fresh apple fritters, are tempting, so I consented and got up. Ok, ladies, I know! I can hear your chuckles and realize I just opened us up to some serious cop donut jokes. I will be the first to agree, you definitely know you are married to a cop when he knows the bakery's hours and you make early morning donut runs together.

We all have our weaknesses and sugary cakes are my husband's. You name it: Twinkies, cookies, éclairs, brownies, and donuts. If it falls in the sweet and bread categories, he is all over it. I am not perfect either. I fall to temptation often and find myself making a pie or banana bread at odd hours or agreeing to go out for ice cream after dinner. I also enjoy one soda every day. I know, not the healthiest habit. But I'm working on it.

The difference between my husband's vice and mine is that he works out regularly and burns those sweets off in no time. He just says he needs to lose a few pounds, and they fall off of him. This is not fair! Men have it so easy.

Saying the word *exercise* makes me cringe. I hate gyms, running, and everything about working out except the comfy workout gear—I could wear that 24/7! I don't get caught up in physical appearances. To me, people with a bit of meat on their bones look better than a waif does anyway. However, I also want to be healthy for my kids and to live a long life, so I must do my part. It is also hard to be married to "McDreamy," who is handsome and fit, when I have gained a few pounds from the holidays and from having three kids.

Maybe your LEO is like mine and does not need to worry about weight. Or maybe he struggles with his weight since he spends a lot of time sitting or eating out. We know that the job can be hard on a diet. That is why it is extremely important to help him in this area. Make healthy choices when you are at the grocery store. Have fresh produce on hand for snacks. Avoid the bakery and candy aisle since you know the goodies will be gone in a few days anyway. Try to go on a walk together a few times a week. Do whatever is necessary to help your LEO's waistline, and your own.

Another great idea is making a meal plan that works with everyone's schedule and cooking the meals yourself. With a little planning and preparation, you can cook a meal in the crockpot for eight hours instead of scrambling to come up with dinner ideas at the last minute when everyone is already hungry. For me, that is when bad food choices and quick decisions to eat out happen, which we all know is not only hard on the diet but also hard on the pocketbook if done frequently.

So make a plan—remember that family calendar we discussed earlier? Ask yourself these questions: When and what are we going to eat? What can be prepared or planned ahead of time? When do we need quick meals? Once you find yourself making healthier meals and wiser food decisions (like no soda during the week or dessert only on the weekends), it will be okay to occasionally treat yourself to that early morning donut date.

A Prayer

Our body is Your temple, God. Help us to take good care of it inside and out. Help me to lead my family in healthy lifestyle choices.

Moments of Truth

What positive things do you already do to keep you and your LEO healthy?

Do you make a meal schedule and exercise together?

What are ways you can improve in this area?

Please write down any additional thoughts or comments.

Today's Action Item

To Do: Go on a walk with my LEO.

I can also:

Day 14

Whatcha Thinkin' About?

14

Whatcha Thinkin' About?

● ● ●

*The LORD would speak to Moses face to
face, as one speaks to a friend.*

Exodus 33:11

I wonder if Moses knew how good he had it! He had honest-to-goodness conversations with the Lord. Sometimes I have pleaded with God to speak to me. He has never answered audibly but has spoken to me in other simpler ways.

Sometimes, I have also begged God to help my husband share his thoughts and feelings with me. Sometimes he can be so silent it drives me bonkers. Do you know what I mean? I am sure you're familiar with the scenario where your LEO is in his own world and is completely oblivious to what else is happening around him—and to what you are saying to him. Seriously, ladies, what planet are they on and where do they go?!

I am a natural talker. I'm the person on the plane who wants to know everything about you by the time we reach our destination. Whereas most people can answer a question in a short sentence, I always go into more detail and end up giving my life story. As you can imagine, it is *very* difficult for me to talk to my LEO when he is not present in the moment. This is what our conversation might sound like.

Me: "How was your day?"   My husband: "Fine."
Me: "Anything going on in the big city?"   My husband: "No."

Then, even though I know he is not paying attention, I will tell him or ask him something, and later he'll have no recollection of it.

One time, just to prove my point, I asked him a question while he was scrolling through his phone. He answered, "Sure. Fine." I started laughing. Then he wanted to know why I was laughing at him. I told him that he had just agreed to us having another baby. He paid better attention the next time we talked, and I learned to wait until he was not as distracted and I had his focus. I've even told him, "I'll wait until you put your phone down and look at me before proceeding with our conversation."

Normally, men are not as talkative as their female counterparts are. LEOs, I have found, are definitely not the touchy-feely types who want to talk about their thoughts or their feelings after a particular situation. So to discover what they're thinking or feeling might be just as unfathomable as having an audible conversation with God.

Although your LEO might not be the talker, it is still important to have an open line of communication with him. When your LEO is too quiet, there might be a bigger issue you need to be aware of. Maybe one reason he's not sharing with you is that he doesn't think you can handle his concerns or that you will be too sensitive to his feelings when he does. Or maybe he doesn't want to stress you out.

Finally, because we are spouses of men who are in very stressful and highly demanding positions, it is extremely important that we watch for signs that our LEOs might be shutting out those around them. In this case, they might be dealing with depression, stress, or anxiety. It is beneficial to know what kind of support and programs are available to us and our LEOs in the event they are needed. Does your department have a chaplain or a counselor? Is there an employee assistance program? Gals, this is so important. You must keep an eye on your officer's mental health!

This breaks my heart, but sadly, statistically LEOs are more likely to take their own lives than to be shot in the line of duty. Never allow it to get to the point where your LEO feels suicide is his only option. As a wife, you have the best insight into your officer's mental health. You know him. Make sure you are available, strong, and focused on your LEO if he wants or needs to talk, and reach out when needed.

A Prayer

Lord, just as You spoke to Moses, help me to have meaningful conversations with my LEO so that I know how he's feeling. Whenever he is struggling, make it clear to me that he needs more encouragement and support.

Moments of Truth

What are some of the ways you and your LEO communicate positively?

Do you have times together when you can discuss feelings, thoughts, and worries?

What can you do to strengthen this area in your relationship?

Please write down any additional thoughts or comments.

Today's Action Item

To Do: Call my LEO instead of texting him.

I can also:

Day 15

How's My Driving?

15

How's My Driving?

* * *

*Whoever heeds life-giving correction will
be at home among the wise.*

Proverbs 15:31

This wouldn't be a true book about law enforcement officers if I do not spend some time on the topic of driving. I think you know what I'm referring to! On the way to church, my husband speeds us along while pointing out cars he would pull over for various reasons. Meanwhile, I silently pray, *God, please don't let us get pulled over on the way to church again.* Yep—he has been pulled over for speeding on our way to church by one of his buddies! Good times, good memories. I swear that every time my husband is in the driver's seat, he thinks he's in his patrol car running through a training course.

LEOs are trained to multitask in their vehicles. They can listen to and answer calls on their radios, watch computer screens, and take sips of their coffee all while driving. However, I don't think my husband needs to do this while he's driving the family around in my mommy mobile. I understand why he does it. I have listened to his argument. He is a professional driver and can do many more tasks in a vehicle than the average citizen. However, he could slow down a bit! We're not in a high-speed chase. I don't know if you've ever been in the passenger seat of this conversation. I once told my husband how I felt about his driving only to receive an evil side glare in return.

And it's not only his driving, ladies. Sometimes when I give him constructive criticism in other areas, he doesn't receive it well. Most wives reading this are confidently nodding their heads in agreement. LEOs are always "right" and know the law, so when they are told they are doing something wrong, they don't seem to take it well. I caution you to tread lightly in this area. LEOs often think they are perfect and never need constructive criticism. They automatically see it as criticism and miss the constructive part.

As spouses, you and your husband are to sharpen each other, make each other better, and point out the things you both need to work on. If this is a difficult area for you, I would like to share a few tips that seem to work for us.

First, try using "I" statements. It's a natural response to feel attacked when someone comes at you with, "You did this," or "You didn't do this." Instead of saying, "You just did XYZ," say, "I feel that a better way to do XYZ is to   " (you fill in the blank), or "Last time I did XYZ, I tried it this way."

Secondly, watch your tone. Remember, LEOs are used to being yelled at or talked to in mocking voices during their shift. They will not respond well to this at home. The few times my tone went up a decimal, I knew my LEO was no longer listening and had tuned me out.

Lastly, I like the saying, "You can catch more flies with honey than vinegar." Maybe you could sweeten the topic or say it in a lighthearted way instead of being so angry or stressed in your response. Remember the words that Mary Poppins sings: "A spoonful of sugar helps the medicine go down." (Insert me singing and dancing!)

Finally, and most importantly, we cannot control how our LEOs respond to criticism from us, even if we give it to them in the most constructive or sugarcoated way possible. What we *can* control is how we respond to constructive criticism that our LEOS give us. We don't need to instantly feel guilty or embarrassed, and we definitely shouldn't make excuses, either. Instead, try thanking him for pointing it out, let it soak in, and try to do better next time. Trust me, if you thank your LEO for his constructive criticism instead of becoming upset, he might be more receptive the next time you tell him to slow down while he races you to church.

A Prayer

Dear God, everyone finds it difficult to receive criticism. Help me to use the right words when I need to guide my LEO and help me to be open to his constructive criticism.

Moments of Truth

Are you better at giving or receiving constructive criticism?

How well do you take it when your spouse points out your errors?

Try thinking of a time when you didn't use the right words to correct your LEO. How could you have reworded it so he would have been able to receive it more easily?

Please write down any additional thoughts or comments.

Today's Action Item

To Do: Thank my LEO when he corrects me.

I can also:

Day 16

When Troubles
Come Our Way

16

When Troubles Come Our Way

● ● ●

The Lord will fight for you; you need only to be still.

Exodus 14:14

Be still. These are only two simple words—but it's so much easier for me to talk about them than to actually do what they say. I am more of a worst-case scenario person. We call them the "what ifs" in our household. What if I cut my finger? What if it gets infected? What if they have to cut it off? What if I cannot type or work anymore? What if I lose my job? What if we cannot make our mortgage payment? What if we lose the house just because of a cut on my finger? I know it seems bizarre, but that is how my mind works. If you will be honest with yourself, there are times you have been guilty of going down the negative "what if" path as well. We let something insignificant become a big deal, and then it causes unnecessary worry and stress.

One day I heard that the school my husband was then working at as a liaison officer was on lockdown. Someone had seen a mentally unstable person in the area with a gun. Before I even knew more details, my mind had gone through the worst-case scenario. In my mind, there was now a school shooting which involved my husband. My stomach churned, and I nervously waited for more news. Thankfully, I received another communication that everything had been resolved. My "what ifs" never occurred, and all that unnecessary worrying was for nothing.

In our husbands' work, troubles will come in many different ways, shapes, and forms. It could be an incident involving officers, a major change in the department, a new assignment, a turnover of coworkers, or different leadership and leadership styles. The list could go on and on. One of the major privileges we have as wives is to be our husbands' cheerleaders and to support them through these troubles and changes.

Recently, after a dangerous situation involving multiple officers,

I heard many wives openly share that they wished their husbands would consider changing careers for the well-being of their family. Then they would not have to worry so much about the safety of their LEOs. This is a good time to remind you that being a LEO is not only a job, but a calling. They do not do this for the money—they know there will be dangers. This is what they have trained or prepared for and, most importantly, this is what they feel God wants them to do. I caution you not to pressure your husband about changing his career. That needs to be his decision or a decision you make together. If you do not support him but instead try to manipulate him and pressure him to turn in his badge, he will regret it and possibly resent you in the future.

No one is promised smooth sailing in this life. We will all go through highs and lows. In spite of this, we can go through whatever struggles come our way *together*. When we get through them, we will be stronger, rely on each other more, and be more resilient for the next storm that comes our way.

As a family, we wanted to establish a tracking system for these highs and lows, so we made a Joshua basket. In the book of Joshua, he talks about letting stones be a witness. The Israelites stacked stones as a reminder of what God had done. I liked this idea, so we placed a wicker basket in a central location in our house to remember important events. We write each event on a stone and place it inside the basket. Here are a few of our stones: my husband's deployment, my husband's police department hire date, the date Grandma passed away, our old addresses, the kid's birthdays, and our wedding date. It is a great way to remember where we have been and what we've triumphed through together.

A Prayer

Lord, help us when troubles come our way. Help us not be overwhelmed during life's highs and lows but, instead, to find confidence in You.

Moments of Truth

How do you help your LEO deal with changes or troubles that come?

List some of the major changes or troubles that you have already overcome together. You may want to create your own Joshua basket.

What is your emergency plan for when trouble comes?

Please write down any additional thoughts or comments.

Today's Action Item

To Do: Take a trip down memory lane and flip through an old photo album.

I can also:

Day 17

Under All That Gear Is a Man

17

Under All That Gear Is a Man

• • •

*Therefore encourage one another and build each
other up, just as in fact you are doing.*

1 Thessalonians 5:11

You have washed his underwear, heard his burps, and smelled his farts . . . glamorous, I know. He is not perfect. Please do not shout "Amen!," because I also need to remind you that you are not perfect either. We all have qualities that probably drive our partners a bit crazy. I heard a saying that I thought was spot on: "We are two imperfect people serving a perfect God." As we go through life together, we will need a lot of love, forgiveness, and patience.

Your LEO is as human as they come. He is also a man who is created in God's image. Sometimes you will like him, and, well, sometimes you won't. Even so, you must remember your place as his partner. You need to build him up and not tear him down. Strive to be his biggest fan and his number one cheerleader. I always try to remember this. Do I always do this? No, but this is a good reminder. I love it when I see ladies saying they back the blue and have their husband's six! This is so encouraging.

There are days when he is really being a man—he can't seem to hang up his towel after a shower even if his life depended on it, he forgets to pick up milk on the way home from work even though I reminded him, or his breath smells bad when he comes in for a kiss. On these days, I try to remember his best qualities—his strong hugs, his loving green eyes, his laughter, and his ability to serve and protect strangers on a daily basis.

One beautiful Saturday morning as I was cleaning the house, I had a mini self-pity party. As I vacuumed rooms between loads of laundry, I found myself grumbling about the fact that I had to do everything around the house and my husband didn't. I thought, *Woe is me. My life is terrible.* Eventually, I snapped out of it and remembered that my husband works one full-time job and is also a part-time serviceman so I can stay home and be more available to our kids, him, and the household. Even though I thought he doesn't do much for me, I began to remember all the things he had done for complete strangers over the years. He had put an arm around a person whose family members had just died, had stayed close to the victim of a car accident, and had taken a troubled teen out for an ice cream. I know, deep down inside, he would do a lot more for me as his bride, his partner, and his wife if I really needed him.

Once, my husband was in a public service announcement where he reminded citizens to lock their cars and not leave them running and unattended because, and I quote him, "No one has a personal police officer." Later, I joked, "I do. I have a personal police officer." My LEO has come to my aid and service many times. I once called him while holding a dying pet, and he came home to be with the kids and me as soon as he was available. Another time, he came home during his break to deal with a suffering mouse in a trap because I could not dispose of the critter. These moments remind me that he would do anything for me, no matter how big or small.

Getting back to the PSA story, what was humorous about him reminding citizens not to leave their cars running and unattended is that shortly after this, my husband left his Jeep idling for six hours overnight. He had started it to let it warm up. Then his plans changed, and he forgot to turn it off. He warmed it up so much that it melted all the snow on the driveway! I laugh as I write this—it's still one of my favorite stories. Moments like these remind us that our LEOs are human and make mistakes. I can laugh with my LEO but not at him (except when he's not around, hehe!).

A Prayer

Thank You, God, for the man You have put in my life. Help me to build him up instead of tearing him down. Help me to always see the best in him.

Moments of Truth

What are some of your LEO's best qualities?

How can you encourage and build him up more?

When was the last time you laughed together? What did you laugh about?

Please write down any additional thoughts or comments.

Today's Action Item

To Do: Hang my LEO's towel up for him without griping.

I can also:

Day 18

Why Can't We Invite Them?

18

Why Can't We Invite Them?

• • •

Have confidence in your leaders and submit to their
authority,because they keep watch over you as those who
must give an account.Do this so that their work will be a
joy, not a burden,for that would be of no benefit to you.

Hebrews 13:17

You are more than halfway through this journey and book. Congratulations! I do hope and pray that you are discovering and learning more about yourself and your LEO. I bet you have also learned a bit more about me too. You've learned that I want to make new friends, I like to host people in our home, and I want people to like me.

When I plan or host events, I enjoy including different types of people. I usually try to incorporate a get-to-know-you activity. Recently, I was planning a house party to kick off the season and wanted to invite a particular police wife I was getting to know. She had kids the same age as ours. When I told my husband about my plans, he reminded me that her husband had recently been promoted to sergeant and that our other friends might be uncomfortable having their superior hanging out with them. I didn't understand the problem but, following my husband's direction, hesitantly did not invite the family. He said we would have more opportunities later to get to know them at set department functions instead of inviting them to our home. He reminded me that I couldn't always include everyone.

A person's rank is not important to me at all but it sure is to my husband. I know this stems from his time in the military as well as with the police department. He is very accustomed to respecting authority and falling in line. He has been trained to know his place. This is a very hard concept for me. I am not familiar with these boundaries. In my world, everyone is on the same playing field and everyone can be my friend.

When we were new to the department, I did not know the rank of many of the officers. As I met their wives, I didn't feel it was important to get their LEOs' rank or title. At one event, I remember spending quite a bit of time talking to the chief's wife. I loved visiting with her. I had seen her a few times at the church we were trying out, and our sons were involved in the same activity. We had things in common to talk about.

Later, someone told me that I was kissing up and shouldn't spend so much time talking to the chief's wife. I thought this was ridiculous and shared my feelings. The fact that a LEO has a few more stripes, bars, or pins on his uniform doesn't make him more important than the other officers. And it certainly doesn't mean I can't visit with his wife.

I have heard from some wives that as their husbands move up the ranks, they become lonelier. The officers feel they cannot fraternize with the subordinates and have admitted to feeling more superior. They then begin to distance themselves from other officers. Soon, they don't feel like they have close friends or other LEOs' families to rely on. I pray you and your officer never get to that place.

Although we need to respect authority, we also need to remember that we are equals. When I run into "higher-ups," I chat with them about neutral topics such as our kids, city events, and so on. In our police department circle, I like to meet new people but also like to learn from those who have been around longer than I have. I am able to glean some wisdom from those who have been in the thin blue line family longer than us.

If you are a new LEOW who is reading this, do not be afraid of rank. Get to know wives who can share their experiences with you. If you are the wife of a senior officer, remember where you came from, remain humble, and reach out to those newer wives. No matter what your rank is, you can always get to know each other and offer support.

A Prayer

Lord, I know You have put individuals in roles of authority. Please help me to respect that but also to treat each person as an equal.

Moments of Truth

What is your LEO's rank?

How can you maintain relationships with individuals when they are promoted? How can you build relationships with those who are new to the department?

Do you think it gets lonelier as you move up the ranks? Or is it lonelier being the new person?

Please write down any additional thoughts or comments.

Today's Action Item

To Do: Reach out to a new wife.

I can also:

Day 19

Don't Be a Statistic!

19

Don't Be a Statistic!

* * *

However, each one of you also must love his wife as he loves himself, and the wife must respect her husband.

Ephesians 5:33

Divorce is never a fun topic. I learned the other day that another LEO's marriage did not make it. This breaks my heart. You may have heard there is an increased risk of divorce within the law enforcement community. I am not sure what to think about this statement. Many of you have been told that because you are married to a LEO your marriage is doomed. However, no matter the career, divorce in general has increased. Don't let this negative thought hang over your marriage.

Some relationships will fail but not solely because they are LEO marriages. I never liked this stigma. Yes, a career in law enforcement is demanding. You and your husband will face struggles that are different from other couples you know, but I am confident you can overcome anything together. I have seen many long, happy marriages that have withstood major circumstances in the law enforcement community. I have heard of couples who have overcome unfaithfulness, financial ruin, and the death of a child. These things are horrible, and couples testify that they are only able to get through them when they include a third person in their marriage. That third person is Christ. He is the only One who can help.

Remember, you are partners in crime *and* partners in life. Together, set up ways to safeguard your marriage. Below is a list of activities proven to help couples feel more connected and assist them through difficult situations:

- Attend church together. If you can't do this due to shifts or scheduling, get involved in a home Bible study. Start one yourself if you need to.

- Read the Bible, a devotional, or uplifting books together.
- Surround yourself with other strong couples and friends.
- Watch movies that challenge you both to grow.
- Stay physically connected. Hug each other daily.
- Go on small retreats or vacations, even if it's only a weekend break from the kids. Time alone is important. I recommend seeking out couples' conferences, which are specifically set up for you to bond and connect with each other.
- Hire a sitter for the evening and spend quality, phone-free time together.
- Be physically active together. Go on a walk or play a sport. There is something about exerting energy together that's good for the soul.

As important as it is to have your own hobbies, interests, and friends, you also need experiences that you can do together. Find your common ground. Make sure this common ground is not your children, because someday they will grow up and start lives of their own. And then what?

Finally, if your marriage needs help or assistance because of physical abuse, substance abuse, or unfaithfulness, you *must* reach out for the necessary professional help. Many departments provide assistance and counseling. You can also seek outside agencies, your church pastor, or the department's chaplain. It is not a sign of weakness to get help. Many LEOs think this way since they are supposed to be the tough one and in control. But the real sign of weakness would be hurting each other, allowing your marriage to fail without doing anything about it, and then becoming a statistic. And, ladies, no one wants that for you, I promise.

A Prayer

Lord, I pray for my marriage. Please keep it safe and make it a testament to other LEO couples. When we encounter challenges, please be the third person in our relationship and may we take our troubles to You.

Moments of Truth

Take a moment to write down your favorite memory from your engagement, wedding, or honeymoon.

What steps can you take to safeguard your marriage?

If your marriage became rocky, who would you talk to or where would you go for help?

Please write down any additional thoughts or comments.

Today's Action Item

To Do: Write a love note to my LEO and hide it in his pocket.

I can also:

Day 20

This Feels Like an Interrogation!

20

This Feels Like an Interrogation!

* * *

Set a guard over my mouth, Lord;
Keep watch over the door of my lips.

Psalm 141:3

Many books have discussed the topic of communication between men and women. Actually, I think the topic must have been examined and etched on stone before paper was even invented! I know you are a smart woman and understand what I mean! Women and men are very different species. Their differences seem to be magnified when they try to communicate with one another. I will say something to my LEO (something I know my girlfriends would *totally* understand), but he acts like I'm speaking another language and he needs an interpreter.

Early in my adult life, I worked in the healthcare industry and traveled giving presentations. One of my favorite sessions was on the topic of communication. I shared how together our tone, body language, and words make up what we are really trying to say. Seriously. Try it. Say, "I like your shoes." Now say it laden with sarcasm, "I like your shoes." Now say it as if you just came across the most gorgeous shoes you have ever seen on a person. "I like your shoes!" I think you get the point.

When you add technology to our communication, you have a another problem or barrier to overcome. Once I texted, "Milk please," to my husband. Simple enough, right? Well, I guess I had already reminded him of this earlier, so when he saw my text, he read it in a nagging voice instead of my sweet, pretty-please voice. We have had a few communication failures over the years. Many of them involve us relying on texts or handwritten notes instead of taking a few more moments to call one another and share a few details.

When it comes to communication, it is also important to remember that our LEOs are lied to, yelled at, and disrespected for a good portion of their days. They are already looking for the bad in people and reading between the lines to discern what is not being said. So they do not want to feel as if they are being treated this way at home.

I also caution you not to tell half-truths. This means only telling him part of the story because you know the other half of the story will start a string of questions. Your LEO is a highly trained professional and can sniff out dishonesty, intimidation tactics, or false statements like nobody's business. Do not make him use his professional skills on you.

However, you also shouldn't feel like a criminal in your own home. Once I had to deal with a situation between our kids that required me to decide on a punishment. Later, my husband kept pressing me to tell him the details. After the fifth question, I asked, "Are you trying to interrogate me?" and "Do you not trust me?" I told him the situation had been handled to the best of my ability. I did not need him to come in and police a situation I felt had been already resolved.

There are going to be communication breakdowns in your marriage, but I encourage you to speak to each other in love and with a gentle tone. We remind our kids to use their special words such as "please," "thank you," and "you're welcome," but do we actually use them on each other? It isn't always possible to do this, but try to treat your LEO like a valued customer or a close friend. Use the words, tone, and body language you would use with that person. After all, he is the friend you will likely have the longest—hopefully for over fifty years or more!

A Prayer

Help me as I communicate with my LEO. May I be polite and respectful. Guide me in my words and tone so we can peacefully share with each other.

Moments of Truth

When is the best time to communicate with your LEO?

How does texting help and hinder your communication with your LEO?

What are some of your favorite *special* words you use on your LEO?

Please write down any additional thoughts or comments.

Today's Action Item

To Do: Speak with love and watch my tone.

I can also:

Day 21

Dealing with a Junkie

21

Dealing with a Junkie

● ● ●

He says, "Be still and know that I am God."
Psalm 46:10

I have never had to deal with a real junkie before. Well, maybe I have and I just didn't know it. A few twitchy or jumpy people have crossed my path. I didn't know if they were on any substance or, if so, what it might be. I cannot spot the signs of a junkie like my husband can. When we go out, he might say, "Our waiter is on something. See how he shakes?" or, "That jumpy person in the corner is on meth." That's when I need to remind him that he isn't at work and needs to quit sniffing out the druggies in the crowd.

I've never used drugs and thankfully have not had to deal with close friends or family members who abuse substances. I am blessed that I do not have experience in this area. The only addiction I have is a daily soda to give me a caffeine rush in the afternoon. Although I am not trained to identify addicts and their drug of choice based on their behavior, I *can* recognize a different kind of junkie. I call them the adrenaline junkies.

Junkies are people who need something to keep them going or gives them a high. Sometimes they are not aware of and cannot control this addiction. Many LEOs become adrenaline junkies to deal with their time outside of work. It can be the rush they get from playing video games or the way they feel after watching the latest action movies and driving fast cars, motorcycles, or boats—whatever they can do to get a rush of excitement in that moment.

Now don't get me wrong, gals. I'm not saying every person that watches an action movie is an addict. What I'm saying is that we all need to make note of what drives us, what fills our time, or what gives us a rush, and ask ourselves, "Do I *need* to feel that way all of the time? Can I leave the 'high' and just be still or calm as the Bible asks us to be?"

Our LEOs live on a different level than the average citizen. They have heightened senses, need to be ready at a moment's notice, with adrenaline pumping, and geared up for action. Sometimes they are in this state so often, it is difficult for them to come down from this sensation and just relax.

It is important to identify when our LEOs are on possible adrenaline highs and to be aware that they cannot maintain this momentum constantly. When they do calm down, most will crash, some will seem depressed, others might sleep much more than normal, and a few will even remove themselves from the unexciting, routine parts of life. They might appear bored with you or seem like they do not care about your day or profession. Sometimes our everyday lives will seem so simple to our LEOs, they won't act interested or excited about us and what we are doing. They do care, but it's just that their minds might be in a different place.

We all need to calm our thoughts and give our minds some peace, especially if we want to live to see retirement. One of your priorities as a LEOW should be to have a calm environment and to provide a relaxing space at home—a retreat from the noise, speed, and high pace of his job. Try dimming the lights, lighting a few candles, and turning down the volume on the television, or better yet, turn it off. My husband once said that he appreciated coming home after a long shift to see the family area tidy with a candle burning. That way, he didn't have to come home to a messy, dark house, even though the rest of us were already asleep. It calmed him and helped him get to bed more easily. It might seem silly to us, but we must help our officers decompress and leave the stress and worries of work at the front door so they can get the rest they need at home.

A Prayer

Lord, help me to know when my LEO is on an adrenaline high so I can help him calm down and get rest and peace. May you give me guidance in ways to help him relax.

Moments of Truth

At home, does your LEO create adrenaline "highs"?

What causes these "highs" for your LEO?

How can you help him calm down and relax?

Please write down any additional thoughts or comments.

Today's Action Item

To Do: Give my LEO a neck rub to help him relax.

I can also:

Day 22

Honey, Who's Our Plumber?

22

Honey, Who's Our Plumber?

● ● ●

Her children arise and call her blessed;
her husband also, and he praises her.

Proverbs 31:28

Proverbs 31 is an excellent passage of Scripture. It tells us about a wife who has a noble character and how she skillfully manages her household and serves her family. I have included the entire passage of Scripture at the end of today's readings. I encourage you to take time to read it, reflect on it, and consider how it can relate to you, your role, and your family.

It is important we take a day on this journey to talk about the household. Since your husband entered law enforcement, you have taken on many household roles and responsibilities—probably more than you originally planned on or prepared for. Maybe you take care of most of the household duties, such as the house, kids, pets, and cars. You might have most things covered or have the phone numbers of those who can help.

Maybe you have become quite handy yourself and can run the lawn mower, weedwhacker, and electric drill. No project is too big or small for you to handle. Some of you ladies might need to rely on family and friends for help because operating power tools is not in your skillset.

Whatever the case, it isn't that your husband cannot do these jobs or does not want to learn how to do them, but most likely, it's because he is too busy. The honey-do list does not ever seem to get any shorter.

Since I have always been a list maker, at times I put a to-do list on our fridge (next to the family calendar) where everyone can see it. Once in a while, a few things get crossed off, but just as soon as one thing is eliminated, another need arises, and I write more items on it. It can be never ending, and to my husband it implies, "You are failing us." We argued about that list enough that we declared it was time to take a break from it! We decided to get some help and just hold off on certain projects—and the to-do list—for the time being.

I get it. My LEO does not have an eight to five, Monday through Friday job. His position is demanding. Depending on the day, the call, or the report that is needed, leaving work on time might not happen. Some weeks, we don't see him for several days. When he is free and at home, he wants to rest, spend time with his family and friends, or do his hobbies. He does not want to fix the garage door.

I learned quickly that I had to help alleviate some of the workload at home, especially if I wanted or needed something done. Either I needed to do it or I needed to find someone to help me. I have also learned to appreciate my husband in other areas. I know he also appreciates me more for dealing with things, such as getting the car's oil changed, taking the pets to the vet for their shots, or finding a repairman.

As a LEOW, you are probably self-sufficient as well. However, it is important to remember that we can't *always* do everything. There are still items that I need my man and his muscles for—like opening that stubborn jar or reaching that high shelf. This assures him that I need his help and value his contributions. But otherwise, I will gladly deal with the garbage, and he will praise me and call himself blessed. I will keep running our household one day at a time.

A Prayer

Lord, help me to handle the household items with a cheerful heart and to remember that my husband is carrying a bigger burden for our family.

Moments of Truth

What are some household tasks that your LEO helps with?

What tasks have you taken over for your LEO?

Can you take on any additional tasks and chores without overburdening yourself? If so, what are they?

Please write down any additional thoughts or comments.

Today's Action Item

To Do: Get the car's oil changed and read Proverbs 31.

I can also:

Proverbs 31

Take a moment to read the entire chapter of Proverbs 31. Then think about the important things that you do to keep your household running efficiently and effectively. The first part is a message to your LEO, and the second part is a description of you!

The sayings of King Lemuel—an inspired utterance his mother taught him. Listen, my son! Listen, son of my womb! Listen, my son, the answer to my prayers! Do not spend your strength on women, your vigor on those who ruin kings. It is not for kings, Lemuel—it is not for kings to drink wine, not for rulers to crave beer, lest they drink and forget what has been decreed, and deprive all the oppressed of their rights. Let beer be for those who are perishing, wine for those who are in anguish! Let them drink and forget their poverty and remember their misery no more. Speak up for those who cannot speak for themselves, for the rights of all who are destitute. Speak up and judge fairly; defend the rights of the poor and needy.

Epilogue: The Wife of Noble Character

A wife of noble character who can find? She is worth far more than rubies. Her husband has full confidence in her and lacks nothing of value. She brings him good, not harm, all the days of her life. She selects wool and flax and works with eager hands. She is like the merchant ships, bringing her food from afar. She gets up while it is still night; she provides food for her family and portions for her female servants. She considers a field and buys it; out of her earnings she plants a vineyard. She sets about her work vigorously; her arms are strong for her tasks. She sees that her trading is profitable, and her lamp does not go out at night. In her hand she holds the distaff and grasps the spindle with her fingers. She opens her arms to the poor and extends her hands to the needy. When it snows, she has no fear for her household; for all of them are clothed in scarlet. She makes coverings for her bed; she is clothed in fine linen and purple. Her husband is respected at the city gate, where he takes his seat among the elders of the land. She makes linen garments and sells them, and supplies the merchants with sashes. She is clothed with strength and dignity; she can laugh at the days to come.

She speaks with wisdom, and faithful instruction is on her tongue. She watches over the affairs of her household and does not eat the bread of idleness. Her children arise and call her blessed; her husband also, and he praises her: "Many women do noble things, but you surpass them all." Charm is deceptive, and beauty is fleeting; but a woman who fears the LORD is to be praised. Honor her for all that her hands have done, and let her works bring her praise at the city gate.

Day 23

I'm Fasting . . . From the News

23

I'm Fasting . . . From the News

• • •

"Even now," declares the Lord, "return to me with all your heart, with fasting and weeping and mourning."

Joel 2:12

When I got online today, the very first thing I saw was an image of a young police officer. It turned out he had been murdered while in his car, just sitting there doing his job. Later I heard on the news that two officers in the South had been shot during a traffic stop. My heart broke when I learned about these tragic and needless deaths. I wondered, *What is happening to our society and country?* I'm sure you've asked yourself the same thing recently.

We know that LEOs often get into dangerous situations, but lately, we hear about more and more senseless crimes against them. Recently, I saw on Facebook three officers holding up signs that said, "Police Lives Matter!" Well, of course they matter! It is tragic that our nation has forgotten that the very people who protect and serve us are now becoming targets for unnecessary crimes and hate.

Sometimes all the news, stories, and pictures are just too much for me. They make me angry. They make me worry. They make me sad. That is when I know I have had enough and need to take a break.

For a while, I had to give up watching the news and reading some articles altogether. There is so much negative news coverage, and to me, the media continues reporting the same negative footage over and over until it becomes ingrained in everyone's minds. At one time, our kids thought that there were multiple riot situations going on after a cop shot a criminal. They were scared that riots would soon begin in our city. I had to assure them it was only one community going through this unfortunate event and encouraged them to pray for that community. Then I had to turn off the news for their sake and mine.

Keeping up with current events and watching the news was helpful in my former job. And it's something I liked to do. However, after I stopped watching the evening news, I noticed I slept better and didn't worry so much about my husband, our community, and our nation. In the long run, taking a break was better for my well-being and helped me be more focused at work, with my family, and during my day.

Have you ever given something up or fasted for a period of time? I have and think it is a good practice to do on occasion. It's a great way to reset our thinking, rely on God, and cut out the unnecessary distractions in our lives.

I have only fasted a few times in my life (from food, soda, wine, and shopping) but have taken longer breaks from TV and social media. A break from any social media is hard for me. I like to keep up with friends, but once people start sharing negative, shock-factor stories, I have to look away. During these times, I try to listen to positive radio like our local contemporary Christian station or listen to an upbeat book on Audible. Better yet, I turn everything off and use that time to calm myself, to enjoy the silence, and to connect with God.

When the news gets to be too much, I encourage you to consider the source of the information. Those who cover stories or comment negatively on LEOs are usually uninformed individuals. Secondly, if it is still getting to you, you may have to turn it off, take a break, or not read it. All of us could do with a little less news. I would encourage you not to get caught up in the stories but instead spend some quiet time with God. And perhaps fast for a week or two and see how you feel.

A Prayer

When the news becomes negative and redundant, Lord, please help me to tune it out for my own well-being and to tune into You instead.

Moments of Truth

How have recent negative events in the media impacted you and your LEO?

How do you filter out the negative stories or comments?

Do you need to do a news or social media fast? If so, what will you take a break from? And for how long?

Please write down any additional thoughts or comments.

Today's Action Item

To Do: Limit my screen time and do something more peaceful.

I can also:

Day 24

My Husband Did *What*?

24

My Husband Did *What*?

* * *

Look to the Lord and His strength; seek His face always.
1 Chronicles 16:11

Once I learned from one of my husband's police brothers about a violent situation my husband had been involved in. I was worried and a bit shaken up and kept my cellphone handy until my husband called to reassure me that all was well. He was fine. Thankfully, it was not a major incident. He had won the day by getting what could have been a bad situation under control, just as he had been trained and prepared to do. Everything went like clockwork. However, as we know, not everything goes perfectly and as planned, especially when our LEOs are dealing with criminals who are running from the law, who are on drugs, or who are mentally unstable.

I know I have mentioned it before and I will say it again—our officers are going to be in violent and dangerous situations. It comes with the territory. They may even have to use lethal force. This reality is why they go through rigorous training and spend hours preparing for the worst, while always hoping for the best. Injuries will occur as well. It is a physically demanding job.

The first time my husband came home with an injury from a criminal, it shocked me and served as a stark reminder that he really was in a dangerous line of work. I'm not talking about pulled muscles and soreness that come with the long hours and physical demands. I am talking about bites, scratches, punches, and cuts—the real deal.

Sometimes it is hard for me to envision my husband running after a person in hot pursuit and then tackling that criminal to the ground. The only tackling I see him doing is in serious tickle fights with our kids. These conflicts end in giggles. I have never seen, nor do I want to see, my husband fighting with a criminal to gain control and make an arrest.

I am grateful that my husband and I can laugh about most of his violent encounters. There is a story about my husband being part of the K-9 unit during a standoff. The criminal was armed and inside his house. When I heard about it, I was confused. My husband does not have a working dog and is not a K-9 officer. They told me he shouted, "Open up, or I'll let the dog in!" and then proceeded to bark like a German shepherd. Whatever works to keep the peace, right? Thankfully, the criminal didn't want to deal with the dog, which at the time was my husband, or with the entire special response team. I am thankful that the situation was resolved due to my husband's quick wit instead of ending with force. It is something we can laugh about now.

I know some of you reading this have had to go through violent situations with your LEO that are not laughable and may still weigh heavily on your heart. Your officer may have had to use lethal force, and both of you may have had to work through him taking a life. What a heavy burden that is to carry for both of you, even if it was warranted and necessary.

I am encouraged that when our LEOs have to go through violent situations, God will be with them and will guide them in their actions. We need to trust that He is in control, and when our LEOs need it, God has even promised extra strength to those who are fighting for good. He will even be present in the fight. And that's better than any backup, if you ask me.

A Prayer

God, please watch over my LEO and keep him safe when violent situations occur. Give him the necessary protection and strength to deal with whatever he encounters.

Moments of Truth

What violent situations has your LEO been involved in?

How did you feel after finding out about these situations?

What can you do to calm yourself so you can focus on his feelings instead of your own?

Please write down any additional thoughts or comments.

Today's Action Item

To Do: Say an extra prayer for my LEO and remind him to be safe.

I can also:

Day 25

God, Are You Serious?

25

God, Are You Serious?

∵

Show me Your ways, Lord, teach me Your paths.

Psalm 25:4

You might be thinking, "Who am I to question God?" I have to tell you, I've been in situations when I had to cry out, "God, are You serious? You want me to do what?" I felt as Moses did before God sent him to tell Pharaoh to free all of the Israelite slaves. Can you imagine Moses's reaction? Maybe it was something like, "Are you kidding? Am I really the best one for this job?"

Have you ever been in a situation or place where you asked God these same questions? Maybe He will challenge you after you go through this journey to do something extra or big among the other LEOWs you are associated with. Maybe He is laying a special burden on your heart even now, such as He did when I knew I needed to write this book. He needs and wants *you* to take action. But, yes, it can be a scary feeling with so much uncertainty when you initiate something new and take those first steps in faith.

I have had similar moments when I knew God was showing me His path and wanted me to follow. It is hard for me when God tells me to do something outside of my comfort zone. I like things to be nice and routine. I do *not* like to be uncomfortable. However, as LEOWs, I believe God will use us in different situations and ask us to step up and help out, even if it is something we'd rather not do.

The first time God sent me on one of His missions, I was terrified. I can remember it as if it was yesterday. Our community had just gone through one of the most tragic events in its history. Three police officers had been shot, resulting in the death of two of them. It was horrible and tragic, but as we know, God has a way of using people during the worst and hardest times.

I felt a bit removed from the grieving families of the officers. We were newer to the department, and I did not have the strong bonds that the other families had, but I still wanted to do something to help and show my support. Over the next few days, some of the strangest coincidences occurred. They pointed me in the direction of helping a family—but not one that you might expect. God wanted me to visit the family of the suspect, the criminal, who shot the officers and who had also died in this tragedy.

As I walked up the steps of this family's house with a box of food, a Bible, a card, and a large watermelon, it probably looked like I was going to a potluck or dropping off a meal to someone who had just had a baby, which I had also done numerous times. But now, I felt as if I was going into the lion's den. It was a powerful visit, and I know God used it for His glory to reach them during a time of confusion, grief, and pain...and to teach me to be obedient.

I firmly believe your husband is not the only one who will be called to do something hard. You will also be used and put to the test. You may be called to put your faith into action if you become aware of a need, whether it is a meal, clothes, or just a hug. You may be asked to go, to put your faith into action, even if you are wondering to yourself the entire time, "God, are You serious?"

A Prayer

God, I wish to be used by You. Help me to be open and willing when You need a pair of hands or feet. Please send me even when is outside of my comfort zone.

Moments of Truth

Have you questioned God's plan when He has called you to action?

What did He want you to do and did you listen?

How can you be more open and willing to serve Him?

Please write down any additional thoughts or comments.

Today's Action Item

To Do: Watch and listen for opportunities to serve.

I can also:

Day 26

Can You Keep a Secret?

26

Can You Keep a Secret?

● ● ●

A gossip betrays a confidence, but a
trustworthy person keeps a secret.

Proverbs 11:13

I admit it; I've let a few secrets slip out before. My bad! Sometimes exciting news has gotten the best of me, and I just had to share it with someone. When someone shares fun news, like an engagement or new pregnancy, it is very hard for me to keep it to myself. I'd like to say that I have gotten better over the years about being discreet. However, instead of keeping their secrets, what is really happening is that I sometimes forget what people have shared with me. Maybe it's good I'm getting forgetful. Many people have told me that I'm a good person to confide in. I want to keep my friends' trust, so I strive to improve in this area. How about you, my friend? Are you good at keeping a secret?

When I was working in the mayor's office, I had access to important information, budgets, personnel documents, big decisions, and more. I didn't like to call them secrets because that made it sound as if the city was keeping things from individuals. Sometimes information was not ready for public release yet, and staff needed to keep things quiet for a bit. I knew a few of these "secrets" about my husband's department. I can honestly say it was awkward knowing something about the police department before he did.

When a new police chief was being appointed, the mayor (my then-boss) was a part of this process and helped select the best candidate—the one who would be my husband's next boss. During this time, my husband and I found ourselves in a difficult situation. Our friends in the police department wanted to know what was happening. I could not tell them and they assumed my husband knew more than he really did. In this particular situation, I felt it best to lay low for a few weeks and avoid large functions where I thought someone might approach me and question me about it. At home, my husband and I agreed the topic was off limits. We still asked each other about our days at work but avoided this particular subject altogether. We did this with mutual understanding, but let me tell you, it was still weird.

The tables have also been turned when my husband couldn't discuss certain situations with me. Once, he had to arrest my friend's husband. He didn't tell me the details. He only said he had to deal with someone I knew. I didn't feel he was keeping secrets from me, but instead, I felt he was being a confidential, reliable source. Later, she shared some of the details and thought it was admirable that my husband hadn't discussed it with me.

Some topics or conversations will be off limits. How do you and your LEO deal with these situations? Can you tell each other everything, or do you have an understanding that your spouse will only tell you the main points? Have you discussed where the line is drawn between keeping secrets and just doing his job?

When you live in a close community or your LEO is part of a smaller agency, secrets can be even more difficult to keep. Recently, someone approached me and said with a little bit of a tone, "Well, I finally met your husband." When I didn't know what she was referencing, she looked confused and asked, "Didn't he tell you what happened?" She assumed he had told me all the details. I told her he couldn't and didn't share everything with me but I hoped her situation, whatever it was, had been handled appropriately. I knew she gained more trust and faith in law enforcement that day. In that moment, I was glad my LEO could keep a secret better than I could.

A Prayer

Lord, help me to be careful with the information that others tell me and to be a confidential source. And help me to be understanding when my LEO can't tell me about a situation.

Moments of Truth

How good are you at keeping secrets?

Can you think of a time when you couldn't share private information? How did you feel? How well did you do?

When your LEO can't divulge information with you, how do you handle this? What topics are off limits?

Please write down any additional thoughts or comments.

Today's Action Item

To Do: Try my best to be trustworthy and keep any secrets I've recently been told.

I can also:

Day 27

Following the Leader

27

Following the Leader

● ● ●

But I want you to realize that the head of every man is Christ, and the head of the woman is man, and the head of Christ is God.

1 Corinthians 11:3

"Follow the Leader" was such a fun game to play on the playground or in the pool when I was little. Even now, I like to play it with my kids while singing, "Following the Leader," the song from the movie *Peter Pan*.

While growing up, I had an older sibling. I liked to follow her lead at home and at school. My sister was a good role model and wonderful big sister. And I wanted to be just like her! When I grew up, I no longer was a follower but, instead, had to step up and be more of a leader. Everyone goes through this natural progression into adulthood. Yet it is helpful for us to remember the importance of being able to follow good leaders even after we've grown up.

I will admit wholeheartedly that it is sometimes hard for me to follow my husband's lead since I handle the majority of our household. I do the finances and pay the bills. I make the yearly plans. I do so much around the house I sometimes forget my husband is the true leader God has placed above our family. To be honest, I don't know why it's so hard for me to let him lead our family. I often have to ask God to help me have a more submissive spirit. My husband is the spiritual leader of the home but I can pray for him more in this role. And when I question his authority, I have to remember that he is always taking charge and leading others in more serious situations at work. He leads trainees. He instructs. He is trained to lead. I can trust him to lead me and our family as well.

When I try to do it all by myself, I sometimes find things do not always work out. It is during what I call these "mommy failure moments" that I am reminded I don't always make the wisest decisions and I should ask for help more often.

It had been one of those days. We were heading home from a late activity when I realized we needed milk (I swear we are always out of milk). I decided to stop quickly at the corner store and run in by myself because it was cold outside. I let our six-year-old stay in the running car and play on my phone—big mistake!

The quick stop took longer than I had planned, and when I returned to the car, my daughter handed me the phone and said someone wanted to talk to me. It was a dispatcher. Oh, my! My daughter had accidentally called 911 and shared that she was alone in a car for a long time. After I explained the situation to the dispatcher, he said he was still going to send an officer out to check the situation. Another, Oh, my! Thankfully, the officer who responded recognized our last name and called me instead of driving out to meet me. This spared me the embarrassment of having to sit in the parking lot and to talk to him in his police car. Thank God!

This situation is a perfect example of how things don't always go as planned, even in those situations where I think I have everything under control. Sometimes, I need help and cannot do everything on my own. I need to rely on others more. I think this is an important lesson for us all, right?

Ladies, once we acknowledge this reality, it's important to trust our co-leader in life, our LEO. He is used to leading and taking control even in the most stressful situations. Even more importantly, it is vital that we trust God with our lives each day. He has promised us that whenever we need help, He will answer us, just like a dispatcher on the other end of a 911 call. I guess what it comes down to is being able to recognize when to be the leader and when to get in line and happily sing, "Following the leader, the leader, the leader!"

A Prayer

God, help me when I am the leader. Let me know when I need to step aside and let my LEO lead. And show us both when we need to call on You for help.

Moments of Truth

Are you a better leader or follower? Why?

How can you empower your LEO to lead?

What are some ways you can show your LEO you rely on him to be the spiritual leader of your household?

Please write down any additional thoughts or comments.

Today's Action Item

To Do: Compliment my LEO on his leadership skills.

I can also:

Day 28

Dealt a Blow

28

Dealt a Blow

* * *

Why, my soul, are you downcast? Why
so disturbed within me? Put your hope in God.

Psalm 42:11

Dealing with disappointment is never fun. The saying "a spoonful of sugar helps the medicine go down" is not always the case (even though it might be helpful when discussing sensitive topics with your LEO, as we discussed on Day 15). No matter how much it's sugarcoated, when life deals us a blow, it is not always easy to swallow.

Due to the nature of the law enforcement field, it might appear that there are more daily discouragements than successes. It is unfortunate that our LEOs will deal with more than their fair share of disappointments. They see, hear, and deal with things many people do not even know are happening in their communities, much less want to know. They deal with people who are going through their worst days. They see the evil side of mankind. My husband has even said that at times he felt he was not only dealing with a person but with an evil spirit inside that person. Oh, my Lord! This is scary stuff!

These low blows can come to our LEOs in many forms, whether it is a breakdown in the system causing a criminal to get off the hook or victims being placed back into the care of the one who has abused them in the first place. It could also be the disappointment of a cold case—the one he could never solve. He also may feel the uneasiness that comes with knowing a dangerous criminal is out there and could strike again. So many LEOs become pessimistic and unable to see the good in people because they repeatedly experience these types of situations.

We know that as long as humans rule this world, systems will fail, bad actions will occur, sin will be present, and people will get away with evil. I once posted this quote from Gandhi on my husband's

Facebook page, "You must not lose faith in humanity. Humanity is an ocean; if a few drops of the ocean are dirty, the ocean does not become dirty," as a reminder that the few individuals he has to deal with do not outnumber the amount of good people in this world.

Some of the disappointments our LEOs experience might be on a smaller scale but still feel like personal blows. Maybe they didn't get an assignment they worked hard for or were overlooked for a promotion. Maybe a close friend left his position or they don't like the way things are currently being run within their department, agency, or division. The list really could go on and on.

There are going to be bad days and even bad weeks. I remember a particularly difficult week my husband had when things were not going well. The morale at the police department was low. He was working through some interpersonal issues, there was a series of challenging calls, and on top of it all, a suspect tried to bite his thumb off. I remember watching him and thinking he was nearing the end of his rope. If I were in his position, I would have had a good cry in the bathtub, drank a glass of wine or ate a tub of ice cream, and held a Netflix marathon. However, that was not him. He kept pressing on.

We are all going to have to go through storms, but we still need to remember to praise God in the rain. These horrible moments, days, or even weeks will help us appreciate the victories. When those good days, successes, and victories come—when he solves the case, catches that criminal, helps that elderly person, and gets that promotion— the success will be even sweeter, and the reward will feel greater. Celebrate these moments together!

A Prayer

Help me, God, to be there for my LEO when he is dealt a blow. Help me not to become negative but to help him see the positive side of the situation.

Moments of Truth

What has been one of your LEO's greatest work disappointments?

How did you help him through that troubled time?

Briefly describe one of the greatest moments of celebration you have shared together.

Please write down any additional thoughts or comments.

Today's Action Item

To Do: Remind my officer about something good happening in the community or at home.

I can also:

Day 29

The Power of Laughter

29

The Power of Laughter

• • •

Our mouths were filled with laughter, and our tongues
with songs of joy. Then it was said among the nations,
"The Lord has done great things for them."

Psalm 126:2

Have you heard the saying, "Laughter is the best medicine"? You've probably found it to be true in your busy, chaotic, and sometimes stressful life. Laughter can relieve pain, refresh spirits, renew minds, and even draw people together. It has many therapeutic purposes. Thank You, Jesus! Often when we go through trying circumstances, though not humorous at the time, we can find their comedic value later.

Life can be serious, and moments in a LEO's day are often very tense. And, like all couples, my husband and I have been through our own difficulties. Having a positive outlook enables us to find something to laugh about afterward. It's good to remember and hold onto these stories that have made us laugh and got us through another day. We continue to laugh about the time my LEO got lost on a call and gave the wrong location for backup, or his high-speed chase after an animal call (the deer that wouldn't die), and an emergency bathroom stop that required lights and a siren. (When you've got to go, you've got to GO!) You get the picture—we all remember painful times but it's just as important to remember the funny ones!

I have been on foreign missions trips and we've also hosted a handful of foreign exchange students from other countries over the years who don't speak our language. Laughter is our universal connection! We are meant to go through life and be in relationships with this powerful form of communication. When people laugh together, they are speaking the same language.

I love the sound of my husband's laughter. He can sometimes be a quiet guy, so when he loudly busts a gut, it's usually a really good one and possibly a bit inappropriate. Whatever caused him to laugh, I know it's needed. It is good for him to laugh and feel that emotional relief.

When you get a group of LEOs together, you hear a lot of laughter. LEOs are known for having a weird or dark sense of humor. They might laugh at odd things that seem crude or rude to the average Joe. And what a LEO finds funny might not amuse the normal citizen. Most of our friends and family would be appalled at the things LEOs find humorous. Even if it seems weird or dark, laughing is still a healthy way to relieve some of the pressures and stresses that come with this calling. Do not be overly concerned about what makes your LEO laugh. As long as he is chuckling, it will get him through another day. And ladies, if things have been tense for too long, find a comedy to watch together or start a tickle fight—do whatever you have to do just to get him laughing!

I believe God created laughter to help us heal, move on, and keep going. Laughter allows us to make light of our circumstances and not take them to heart. It is important to remember this fact, to take time to find the funny moments, and to laugh with your LEO, even if it means finding his tickle spot or being a bit silly.

A Prayer

Thank you, Lord, for laughter! Give us moments in our days to laugh together so we can get through anything. Remind us of the funny moments from the past.

Moments of Truth

What kind of humor do you and your LEO enjoy? And what makes you laugh?

Recall a funny story that both you and your LEO still find humorous.

How has laughter helped you both through stressful times?

Please write down any additional thoughts or comments.

Today's Action Item

To Do: Share a funny meme with my LEO.

I can also:

Day 30

He's My Hero

30

He's My Hero

* * *

Humble yourselves, therefore, under God's mighty hand, that He may lift you up in due time.

1 Peter 5:6

When I tell my husband he is my hero, he thinks I'm joking, but I'm not. He really is my hero. Growing up, I didn't know my father and didn't have many strong male role models in my life. When I tell my husband he is my hero, it is a true statement. I like to remind him of it often. At times, I'll sing lyrics from "Wind Beneath My Wings" by Bette Midler: "Did you ever know that you're my hero . . .," and he'll just roll his eyes at me and laugh. However, it is true, and I want him to know it!

One day, I heard about a LEO's high-speed pursuit of an armed and dangerous individual. It was on the news and on social media. "Who was the officer involved?" I asked. I was surprised to find out it was my honey. He was the one who saved the day! He called me later, his adrenaline still pumping, and gave me brief details. Next time when I saw his superiors, they praised him. They asked me about the incident and if my husband had mentioned it. My LEO did tell me about it but hadn't made it sound as exciting as others did because he was just doing his job. To him, it was another day in the life of a cop.

One Christmas, the kids got him a sign with their own money. They were so cute and so excited about their gift. It read, "Real heroes don't wear capes, they wear badges." He was appreciative but didn't want to hang it in his man cave or office. He felt it would be boastful to do so and didn't view himself as a hero. Even when he was deployed and serving our country, he didn't like us to refer to him as a hero. Again, he was just doing his job. To him, heroes are people we read about in books or watch in movies, not a guy from the Midwest.

I had to encourage him and remind him that it's good that the kids and I see him as our hero. He is our family's superhero. It's healthy for us to get excited about what he is doing. He's fighting evil with good. He's serving, protecting, and going where most people would not go. He's helping the people who most of us would ignore or walk away from. I also need to remind him that he doesn't have to be perfect all the time or save the day every day. We will be proud of him no matter what.

Sometimes it's the small things, my friend. He is also my hero and saves the day when he works for hours to get our cat out of a tall tree, removes a bad splinter out of a kid's foot, or gets up with the baby so I can sleep. That's true gallantry. These little things make him a hero in my eyes as well, not just the big things that make the headlines.

Gals, be proud of your husband and that you are a LEO family. Of course, we want to be careful not to allow our pride for our LEOs to cross into boastfulness, but it's always important that we remind our LEOs they are special and we are proud of them for the little things and the big things. They can always use more encouragement, especially from us! Take a moment to think about what has set your LEO apart and made him a hero!

To the tired officer who works long hours to look for a lost boy . . . you are a hero. To the officer who puts on his uniform every day even though he suffers from physical ailments . . . you are a hero. To the officer who pulls the lifeless child out of the pool and cries later . . . you are a hero. To the officer who pulls the trigger when he is attacked by a criminal with a weapon . . . you are a hero. To the officer who is a minority and is ridiculed by his own people but still does the work . . . you are a hero. To the officer who holds and prays with a new widow in the ER waiting room . . . you are a hero.

A Prayer

Lord, thank You for giving me a hero to root for. Help me not to be boastful of his position. Instead, help me remind my LEO of the important work he is doing.

Moments of Truth

When you were growing up, who was your hero? Why?

How do you show your LEO that you are proud of him?

What are some of your LEO's most amazing moments or noteworthy accomplishments?

Please write down any additional thoughts or comments.

Today's Action Item

To Do: Write my LEO a note of encouragement.

I can also:

Day 31

You Are Wonder Woman

31

You Are Wonder Woman

● ● ●

For the Spirit God gave us does not make us timid,
but gives us power, love and self-discipline.

2 Timothy 1:7

We are almost at the end of our journey together. I'm so proud of you for taking the time to go through these topics. I hope you have laughed, been challenged, and shed a few tears but, above all, I pray you have been encouraged in your important role as a LEO wife. We've spent so much time talking about your husband, his roles, how amazing he is, and how you can better help him. But now I feel we have saved the best topic for last. Today we talk about *you*! Yes, *you*, my friend!

Did you know that you're a superhero as well? Seriously! LEOWs are like Wonder Woman, juggling work, life, kids, pets, the house, and other stressors. But let's be honest—I know you have days where you feel you've failed. Maybe you struggle with your husband's role and feel selfish. Maybe you wish he would do something safer than law enforcement. Maybe, at this exact moment, your house is an absolute mess and you wish you had it all together. Maybe your kids are screaming at each other, and you feel you are as far away from being a role-model family as you can be. Maybe, just maybe, you are reading this from the bathroom just to escape everyone!

We will have these moments and feelings, but I firmly believe God put you in this specific place—a Law Enforcement Officer Wife—for a reason. He has an individual purpose for you. The fact that you have spent time going through this journey shows how serious you consider your role of supporting your LEO and being a better wife, which is awesome! Cheers to you!

It is sometimes hard for me to accept compliments. I get embarrassed or think, "Yeah, right." We are all our own worst critics.

However, today, I need you to put away your shyness, not be so hard on yourself, and soak up this compliment: You are amazing! One more time—YOU ARE AMAZING! (Yes, I am shouting this at you!)

You have earned superstar status. You've endured countless sleepless nights. You have been flexible with your schedule. You have been stood up on dates. You have had more plans fall through than can be counted. You have offered up countless prayers of safety and protection. You have cried tears and felt heartache when something tragic has happened in your community. You have felt fear when another LEO has demonstrated the ultimate sacrifice by giving his life in the line of duty. You have worried. Only *you* could have endured these things, gone about your day, and still been there mentally, emotionally, physically, and spiritually for your family and your LEO.

Remember the Proverbs 31 chapter you read on Day 22? If not, read it again. You should make your own list of everything you do, and I know it would be praiseworthy. I encourage you to do something special for yourself. Celebrate who you are and where God has you. It is not a mistake or a coincidence. You are at this place in your life for a very specific reason.

Lastly, even though you are Wonder Woman, you still need more superpowers—the type of powers that can only come from a relationship with Christ. Let Him be on your team and rely on Him. I know you will be able to get through anything together.

A Prayer

God, thank You for taking me on this journey. Help me to apply what I've learned. Thank You for the gifts and abilities You've given to me. I pray I will use them to help my LEO and for You!

Moments of Truth

Are you good at receiving compliments? Why or why not?

What things are you most proud of about yourself?

How do you remind yourself that you are amazing, and how do you treat yourself?

Please write down any additional thoughts or comments.

Today's Action Item

To Do: Recharge my own superpowers with extra prayer (and maybe some shopping!).

I can also:

Conclusion

Our journey together is complete! (I'm happy, but a little sad, too.) You covered a variety of topics and went through many moments of truth that will help you stay encouraged and support your LEO. I hope you feel refreshed, renewed, and recharged for this special mission and role.

I wish I could give you more words of encouragement but, instead, I pray that God will use my goofy stories, mommy mishaps, and random adventures for His Glory. Healing needs to take place in the law enforcement community, and I strongly believe the healing will come from within the home and from the family.

I tried not to give too many military examples and stories from my husband's experience with the South Dakota National Guard, but did want to share a piece from a presentation I created and shared with military police wives. It is called the *Top 10 Tips to Survive a Deployment.* I feel that our journey can also be summed up in these ten tips.

1. Make a plan with your LEO for as many aspects of life as you can, such as family schedule, meals, or worst case scenarios. Have something in place.
2. Set up a budget. Many couples fight about money. You have enough stress, and this doesn't need to be one of them.
3. Be positive. When things get tough and the media floods you with negativity and instills fear, remain unwavering in your husband's calling. Be confident in God's plan for both of your lives.
4. Keep busy. Do not spend free time worrying. Instead, have hobbies and projects that focus your mind on positive things.
5. Be flexible. Plans are going to fall through, and expectations won't always be met. Remember to have grace and go with the flow.
6. Ask for help. You don't have to do everything and don't need to do it alone. Reach out to friends and family for assistance and emotional support.

7. Keep your lines of communication open with your LEO. Having more information is better than not having enough or bottling everything up inside.

8. Take care of yourself. Your family and your LEO need you to be well in all areas of your life.

9. Keep the faith. Seek God and His guidance during the ups and downs of life. He will be there for you, no matter what.

And last, but not least,

10. Stay connected. Be involved. Do things with other wives, attend department functions to know what's going on, and know the resources that are available to you. But most importantly, stay connected to your LEO.

I would like to leave you with one final story. A few years ago, my husband and I attended a military ball as special guests of our friends. It was a grand affair, and my husband got the night off for it. I bought a new ball gown and sparkly shoes. My husband wore a new suit. We were looking good!

For a moment when we were there, I felt as if we should dress up and attend grand galas more often—until my husband's phone alarm went off during the opening remarks being made by a military dignitary. We had both silenced our phones, but he'd forgotten about the alarm to wake him up to get ready for work. We tried not to laugh but couldn't help letting out a giggle. We had to laugh. This was our life. Normally he'd be waking up about now having a bowl of cereal while the kids and I got ready for bed. Instead, we were having a night out like real adults together. When does real adult time even happen?!

We finally regained our composure as the governor took the podium. He told a story that I will never forget. He shared how he and his wife of many years were at an event and ran into her old high school sweetheart. Unfortunately, the years had not been the best to this man. He was unsuccessful, a bit out of shape, and not well-groomed. Later, the governor jokingly said to his wife, "Just think, you could have been married to him." Do you know how she responded? She said, "Then he would have been governor and you would have turned out like him."

We all laughed, but the governor admitted it was true. Behind every man, especially the strong, successful ones, is a good woman who has supported him and helped shape him into who he is today.

This is especially true in law enforcement. Behind the most grounded and successful officers are their amazing wives. They need us. We have their six; we back the blue! Together, we are a team! They might not always tell us this or acknowledge all that we do, but it is undeniably true. Your LEO, his department, your community, and the nation are better because of what you do behind the scenes for your officer. You are amazing! Keep up the good work. God bless you, my friend.

Letter to Readers

Dear Friend,

 I want to take these last moments together to get real with you. Super real!

 There are days that I am so proud of being an officer's wife. So stinkin' proud!

 I could redecorate our family room with cute thin blue line things and rock the cute t-shirts that pledge my allegiance and put decals on our cars so everyone knows we are a police family.

 Seriously, don't mess with me—my husband is a cop! And I'm proud and loud about it!

 Then there are other days.

 Days I'm sick of this life and I'm tired. Days I don't want this burden.

 These are the times that I really question my husband's calling and think he could be doing something safer, something that allows for more family time, and something that makes more money to support our family.

 I have doubts.

 I don't always have it together.

 My mascara gets clumpy. My lipstick smears.

 Dishes, laundry, and dirty diapers fill my days.

 I make mistakes all the time. I'm not perfect.

 But it is on these days that I am reminded that God loves me and that He is perfect.

 I don't need to be.

 You, my friend, don't need to be either.

 God has a plan. A plan for us all.

 God's plan for my husband and me on this crazy LEO journey is PERFECT.

 I'm so thankful you and I have had this time together. I don't know about you, but there's times I feel like I'm going on this LEOW journey all by myself. Although I have some amazing RCPD wives to talk to, I still need to be reminded that I am not alone in my struggles, worries, and fears.

 You are not alone either.

I know I've talked a lot about Jesus in this book and some of you were prepared for it because you knew it was going be a devotional book before you even cracked it open.

However, some of you were a little caught off guard by some of my prayers, statements, the verses used, and how often I mentioned we need God.

Maybe this book has made you reevaluate your own spiritual life and you need to take a moment to connect or re-connect with your first Love—your Maker.

Our husbands aren't perfect, but there is one who is. And that's Jesus Christ, who died for you. He really is the One that has helped me through this journey. And I praise God for my personal relationship with Christ.

I don't know where you are with this.

Maybe you need to take a moment and say these words to God,

"I thank You, God, for your son Jesus and that He came to earth to die on the cross to wash away my sins. I am sorry for the times I've tried to do life alone, when I make mistakes, when I'm boastful and I think I can do this all by myself. Now I turn to you. I leave my sins at the cross. Please help me to live each day for You. I give my life to You."

Now maybe you've said that prayer before and you need to say it again and re-commit your life. I encourage you to do that as well.

God knows your heart.

And don't feel like you need to use my words, just speak from your heart.

Now, tell a friend!

No matter how late it is, call them or text them and let them know that you accepted Christ or you re-committed your life to live for Him because you know it will help you no matter what comes your way as the wife of a law enforcement officer.

Seriously, do it!

Email me too! I'd love to celebrate with you!

Again, thanks for taking the time to go through this book with me. I pray it has helped you as a LEOW.

You are amazing.

You are loved.

Your sister in Blue and in Christ,
Mrs. 659
Jessica Mertz

Extra Questions for Group Study

How did *Moments of Truth* strengthen you as a LEOW?

Did going through this journey help your LEO as well? If so, how?

Did you perform the action items along with each day's reading? If so, how did your LEO respond to them?

. . . .

. . . .

. . . .

. . . .

. . . .

. . . .

. . . .

. . . .

. . . .

. . . .

If you could write another day's topic of discussion, what would it be and why?

. . . .

. . . .

. . . .

. . . .

. . . .

. . . .

. . . .

. . . .

. . . .

. . . .

. . . .

Is it easier to go through this type of a book alone, with a friend, or in a group?

Which day's topic got the most discussion or raised the most questions and why?

Additional Resources

A CHiP on my Shoulder: How to Love Your Cop with Attitude by Victoria M. Newman

Bullets in the Washing Machine by Melissa Littles

Courageous (film) directed by Alex Kendrick

Devotions and Prayers for Police Officers: Providing Meaningful Guidance in a Variety of Situations by Steve J. Voris

Financial Peace: Restoring Financial Hope to You and Your Family by Dave Ramsey

Fireproof (film) directed by Alex Kendrick

Girl, Wash Your Face by Rachel Hollis

I Love a Cop: What Police Families Need to Know by Ellen Kirschman, PhD

Laugh Your Way to a Better Marriage by Mark Gungor

Lives Behind the Badge and *Survival Guide for Police Wives* by Kristi Neace

Living Well Spending Less: 12 Secrets of the Good Life by Ruth Soukup

Love and Respect: The Love She Most Desires; The Respect He Desperately Needs by Dr. Emerson Eggerichs

One Month to Live: Thirty Days to a No-Regrets Life by Kerry and Chris Shook

The Bible, New International Version

The 5 Love Languages: The Secret to Love That Lasts by Gary Chapman

The Crazy Lives of Police Wives by Carolyn Whiting and Carolyn LaRoche

The Love Dare by Alex Kendrick and Stephen Kendrick

The Power of a Praying Wife: Prayer and Study Guide by Stormie Omartian

The Purpose Driven Life: What on Earth Am I Here For? by Rick Warren

Acknowledgements

Expressing my overwhelming thanks to all of those who helped make this book a reality is like standing in the middle of a massive greeting card aisle, reading dozens of beautiful sentiments but still not finding the exact card. The perfect words elude me! But I have to decide on something, I must try . . . so here goes.

I would like to give a special thank you to all of my sisters! My sister by birth, Jamie; my sister in Christ, Mandi; and my sisters with the Rapid City Police Department—Jo, Kyla, Melea, Shelley, Sarah, Kirstin, Danielle—I could not have written this book without your example and the inspiration you give me. I am grateful to be surrounded by so many amazing women!

To Dan, my man, thanks for believing in me and being so patient with me as I worked on this book—I have the best hubby!

To my mom, Lora, I get my creativity from you. Thanks for encouraging me to always keep pushing forward!

To Zac, Gabby, and Izzy, thanks for being understanding of your momma's work time and for being the best LEO kids ever!

A special shout-out to Kyla and Carly for spending many hours together as we shaped this book in its early stages—thank you, ladies! This project would not have got rolling if it weren't for your ideas and support. And to the ladies who prayed, asked how the book is coming along, and kept me going, I am so appreciative of you—Teri, Laura, Megan, Donna and Katie—thank you all!

A special thanks to my professional team that helped get things finalized!

Kristina, thank you for all of our coffee and lunch dates as we went page by page through this book—you are one of the most patient people I have ever met, and that's what makes you such a great editor!

Kris, thank you for designing, redesigning, and redesigning again the perfect book cover. I seriously think I emailed you 1,000 times and you always kept encouraging me despite my changes.

Henry Roy, thank you for making me look more amazing than I am in person in my professional headshot—you are one talented photographer!

Tim, thank for your vision and patience as we waited to get the perfect book cover shot while the sun was setting over Rapid City—your prayers for this project were appreciated.

Jeff, thanks for being my technical guy and getting the website up and going—I appreciate how understanding you are to my many crazy ideas!

To all of those that kept me, my family, and this book in your prayers during its creation—your support has undeniably made a difference.

And lastly, and most importantly, I thank God for placing this idea on my heart even if it meant many sleepless nights wrestling through my own moments of truth. It will all have been worth it if it helps one other LEO wife!

About the Author

Jessica Mertz is the proud wife of a military and civilian police officer. Her husband, Dan Mertz, wears two uniforms, that of a South Dakota National Guard Military Police Officer and that of a Rapid City Police Officer.

Jessica is involved in her community, serves in various ministries, and is active in her church. Known as the stay-at-home mom who's never home, Jessica's three children, Zachary, Gabrielle, and Isabelle, keep her on the go. When free time allows, she enjoys a good DIY project, spending time in the beautiful Black Hills, and a little retail therapy.

Jessica holds a master's degree in mass communications with an emphasis in public relations and marketing from the University of South Dakota. She's always up for a challenge and learning something new.

Jessica loves to hear from her readers, especially stories from fellow law enforcement officer wives. You can contact her at LEOWmoments@gmail.com.

She would also love the opportunity to come to your community to speak and encourage other LEO wives. Find out more details by visiting www.momentsoftruthbook.com.

Printed in the United States
By Bookmasters